THE DYNAMICS OF PREVENTIVE DIPLOMACY

AF662596

THE DYNAMICS OF PREVENTIVE DIPLOMACY

RANJIT SINGH KALHA

KNOWLEDGE WORLD

KW Publishers Pvt Ltd
New Delhi

in association with

United Service Institution of India
New Delhi

2011 FPBA BEST PUBLISHERS AWARD (ENGLISH)

KW Publishers Pvt Ltd
4676/21, First Floor, Ansari Road, Daryaganj, New Delhi 110002
✉ knowledgeworld@vsnl.net ✆ +91.11.23263498/43528107

www.kwpub.com

All rights reserved. No part of this book may be reproduced or transmitted in any form or by any means, electronic or mechanical, including photocopying, recording or by any information storage and retrieval system, without permission in writing.

ISBN 978-93-81904-97-8

© 2014, United Service Institution of India

Published by Kalpana Shukla, KW Publishers Pvt Ltd
4676/21, First Floor, Ansari Road, Daryaganj, New Delhi 110002

Printed and bound in India

This book is dedicated to my children

Manjit and Diviya

Baljit and Anika

Contents

INTRODUCTION

Ever since the end of the cold war the concept of preventive diplomacy has gained widespread traction. From simply being an effort to prevent super power collision, it has assumed a much wider definition and even gone to the extent of ushering in the concept of 'R2P'[Responsibility to Protect]. This new activism has led to international concern that unbridled 'R2P' would result in the interference in the internal affairs of nation states and could be the precursor of new found 'colonialism.' This sense of alienation is most acute amongst newly independent states that having shed old style colonialism did not want yet another form to be introduced in the form of assumption by some powers of the right to interfere in their internal affairs.

Nevertheless there is a pervasive feeling that in the modern world no one should be allowed to get-away with heinous crimes against humanity, including crimes against a section of society within a nation state. Therefore it was felt that there is an urgent need for evolving a code of conduct and that this code must have international sanction. Of particular interest is the fact that any interference in the internal affairs of a nation state must be under international supervision, internationally acceptable and certainly under well- defined parameters. There should be no open ended intrusion; which therefore suggests that it should be terminated as quickly as possible consistent with the well-defined objectives.

There is also the concern within the international community that problem areas and issues that are likely to cause international tension must be anticipated and attended to before they assume alarming proportions. That in essence is the concept of taking action at the incipient stage or preventive diplomacy.

Mr. R S Kalha has done a very useful study of all these issues and included in his study are case studies of some recent crisis situations that show how important it is for the international community to anticipate and deal with issues before they escalate to cause acute international tension. The study also establishes that international action has been successful where there has been international unanimity on the action to be taken. Of particular note is the fact that it is essential that all the great powers must be of one view. Any dissonance amongst them invariably irretrievably cripples any international effort. Thus it is still old fashioned great power politics that holds sway.

The book is the result of research fellowship under the MEA Chair awarded to Mr. R S Kalha by USI for 2012-13.

Lieutenant General **P K Singh**
PVSM, AVSM (Retd)
Director, USI

CHAPTER ONE

WHAT IS THE MEANING OF PREVENTIVE DIPLOMACY?

Whenever the issue of preventive diplomacy is raised or discussed one fundamental question that is often asked is what do we mean by preventive diplomacy? Is it simply the absence of conflict or are there more enduring and comprehensive definitions. How is it any different from normal conventional diplomacy? Normal conventional diplomacy is not time specific for it is engaged in by most nation states on every suitable occasion and is a continuous process. One scholar has described the difference between preventive diplomacy and normal diplomatic practice in that "it's time frame is medium or short term and that it operates in an environment where the intensity of conflict is still moderate."[1] On the other hand, some feel that Preventive Diplomacy must be in general "informal, low key, non-binding, non-judgemental, non-coercive and confidential"[2] and that the main focus of preventive diplomacy is to identify and respond to looming conflicts in order to prevent the eruption of violence. In principle the main argument in favour of preventive diplomacy is based on the belief that it is better if conflicts are "cured" before they become "fierce".

This argument also looks at the cost-benefit dimensions: once a vicious conflict has erupted, it is extremely difficult to bring it to an end. Other interpretations—like that of Bruce W. Jentleson—see preventive diplomacy as characterised by its function of excluding the occurrence of violence in opposition to war diplomacy; which is supposed to be mainly directed at limiting or terminating violence. Most renowned scholars on the subject therefore, it would seem, are divided and more often than not several differing definitions of preventive diplomacy are available. Some differences are merely of nuance, some are substantive. Therefore, it is important to scrutinise each with care before any definitive conclusions can be drawn or a general consensus arrived at in finding the most appropriate definition.

When the UN Charter was negotiated and finalised soon after the conclusion of the Second World War, the emphasis was on "collective" action to ensure peace. It was only in the 1960s that the then-UN Secretary-General Dag Hammarskjold, who was one of the first to use the term "preventive diplomacy," broadened the scope and argued that the goal of preventive diplomacy was "to keep local conflicts from being entangled in superpower rivalry."[3] According to Hammarskjold, the twin objectives of preventive diplomacy were to keep "newly arising conflicts outside of bloc differences and in the case of conflict on the margin of, or inside the sphere of bloc differences … to bring such conflicts out of this sphere through solutions … [aimed at] … their strict localisation."[4]

In Hammarskjold's view preventive diplomacy then included the following instruments: hotlines, risk-reduction centres, and transparency measures. These instruments were intended to help recognise and fill any power vacuum in order to prevent the United States or the Soviet Union from taking actions that could escalate conflicts and lead to a nuclear confrontation.[5] Thus Hammarskjold's view of preventive diplomacy was largely based on the need to prevent a conflict between the then two superpowers. With the end of competition between the US and the Soviet Union as the Cold War came to a close, Hammarskjold's conceptualisation of preventive diplomacy, as basically the prevention of conflict between the two superpowers, was thus rendered as less than relevant.

The end of the cold war signalled that the concept of what constituted preventive diplomacy, needed a wider and perhaps a new definition. This was provided by the then UN Secretary-General Boutros Boutros-Ghali in 1992, in his seminal work *An Agenda for Peace: Preventive Diplomacy, Peace-Making and Peace-Keeping.* In it Boutros-Ghali defined preventive diplomacy as an "action to prevent disputes from arising between parties, to prevent existing disputes from escalating into conflict and to limit the spread of the latter when they occur." Boutros-Ghali's view was much broader than that of his predecessor and was not limited to securing peace between the two superpowers only. It was a world view that encompassed almost each and every situation. It was also the time when the world no longer seemed to be divided into two competing power blocs. The possibility therefore arose that states, hitherto bitterly divided, could work together for the common good of humanity and to eliminate the scourge of conflict. Boutros-Ghali's definition was one such an attempt to bridge the divide and arrive at a common understanding.

In 2001 the then UN Secretary-General, Kofi Annan proposed that "preventive diplomacy" be renamed as "preventive action." For him preventive diplomacy was a method for preventing human suffering and also as an alternative to costly politico-military operations. He also felt that other forms of "action," that could have useful preventive results, should also be given priority. For instance, preventive deployment, preventive disarmament, preventive humanitarian action, and preventive peace building, which involved the consent of the government or governments concerned, as well as a wide range of actions in the fields of good governance, human rights, and economic and social development. For this reason, Annan decided to rename "preventive diplomacy" as "preventive action." It is of interest to note that he emphasised that "preventive action" should be *limited* (emphasis added) mostly to measures stipulated under Chapter VI of the UN Charter, but also noted that enforcement action as provided under Chapter VII of the UN Charter must remain a legitimate means of last resort in order to prevent massive violations of fundamental human rights or other serious threats to peace.[6]

The present UN Secretary-General, Ban Ki-moon went even further in redefining preventive diplomacy. Ban Ki-moon emphasised three points. Firstly, he advocated the strengthening of UN "partnerships" *with all stakeholders* (emphasis added). He felt that successful preventive diplomacy would require contributions of a range of actors, at both the regional and international levels. Secondly, it should be ensured that developments include the increasing use of international contact groups. Progress can only be achieved through "partnerships" that yield a combination of influence, impartiality, capacity and capability. Effective preventive action depends critically on the willingness of the parties in the conflict to engage. Neighbouring countries and sub-regional organisations could exercise a unique influence, and perhaps serve as key allies. Thirdly, the international community must continue to invest in prevention. The global economic crisis has put new pressures on resources, and there is an overall trend towards doing more with less. Diplomatic approaches and responses, when successful, have to be highly cost-effective. Fourthly, the UN ought to support and encourage the role of women in preventive diplomacy. The Security Council Resolution 1325, reaffirms the important role of women in the prevention and resolution of conflicts and yet women are still under-represented in the formal stages of conflict prevention.[7]

It must be noted however that almost all UN Secretaries-General have emphasised that any "preventive diplomacy" undertaken *must be within the ambit of the UN Charter and that State sovereignty must not be violated* (emphasis added). It was only later that the concept of "responsibility to protect" (R2P) was introduced, which in a sense diluted state sovereignty and created a scope for "interference" in the internal affairs of a nation state.

While the definitions of preventive diplomacy were being refined at the international level, regional initiatives in this regard were also being undertaken. In Africa, the notion of "non-interference" has largely been replaced by the principle of "non-indifference" to imminent threats to peace, security and the unconstitutional changes of government. In the Americas, for example, the OAS has made the prior resolution of differences a priority before it leads to a conflict. In the Pacific region, the Biketawa Declaration of the Pacific Island Forum in 2000 provided a framework for settlement of disputes and early diplomatic response to emerging security situations. The ASEAN Regional Forum (ARF) built on the definitions provided by the then UN Secretary-General Boutros-Ghali. However because of its very nature, its initiative was regional in its scope. The ASEAN (ARF) approach included some very general principles that it felt constituted preventive diplomacy. Since the ARF is a regional organisation its definitions are, but naturally, of relevance mainly in the regional context. The ARF principles were:

- preventing severe disputes and conflicts from arising between States which pose a serious threat to regional peace and stability;
- preventing such disputes and conflicts from escalating into armed confrontation; and,
- limiting the intensity of violence and humanitarian problems resulting from such conflicts and preventing them from spreading geographically.

The ARF was also keen to emphasise that its definition was mainly centred on the peaceful aspects of preventive diplomacy and did not relate at all to any military or military induced coercive methods. It therefore emphasised that:

- Preventive diplomacy is about diplomacy. It relies upon diplomatic and peaceful methods such as persuasion, negotiation, enquiry, mediation, and conciliation.
- It is voluntary. Preventive diplomacy practices are to be employed only at the request of the parties or with their consent.
- It is non-coercive activity. Acts that require military action or the use of force, or other coercive practices, such as sanctions, are outside the scope of preventive diplomacy.

- It requires trust and confidence. The facilitator or mediator in the dispute must be seen as trustworthy and as an impartial honest broker by all involved parties.
- It rests upon international law. Any action should be in accordance with the basic principles of international law.
- It is based on respect for sovereignty and non-interference in the internal affairs of a State. This includes the principles of sovereign equality and territorial integrity.
- It requires timeliness. Action is to be preventive, rather than curative. Preventive diplomacy methods are most effectively employed at an early stage of a dispute or crisis.

The above principles and similarly-worded definition and principles of preventive diplomacy were incorporated into the July 2001 ARF Chairman's Statement and included in the Charter of ASEAN that was concluded in 2007. All these manifestations contained in the regional organisations' charters are reflective of the broad approach that emerging security concerns must be addressed, in a timely manner, within the appropriate regional mechanisms devised for the purpose. It was also the general feeling that such issues, if dealt with at the regional level had a greater chance of success than dealing at the international level, where such issues tend to be treated as being rather remote.

Not only have regional initiatives emerged, but national effort by individual states has also taken root. For example, the United States and particularly during the term of the Obama Administration, in its "national security strategy" policy paper highlighted the importance of preventing violent conflict and conflict prevention has been identified as a priority function for the newly established

Bureau of Conflict and Stabilisation Operations. The US administration has also set up the Atrocities Prevention Board (APB) with a mandate to stop genocide and Human Rights abuses *before* they begin. Similarly, other national efforts have also been developed by emerging economies such as BRICS.[8]

Other eminent scholars have defined preventive diplomacy in much more broad terms than done hitherto. They have identified preventive diplomacy as "action taken in vulnerable places and times to avoid the threat or use of armed force and related forms of coercion by states or groups to settle the political disputes that can arise from the destabilising effects of economic, social, political, and international change."[9] The clear implication being that preventive diplomacy would inevitably include the use of force or the threat of the use of force. This "muscular" view of preventive diplomacy is at odds with the earlier view that preventive diplomacy represented only "soft" mediation. Nevertheless there is also the view that in the contemporary world the maintenance of peace occupies the primary and essential space and therefore preventive diplomacy requires a different kind of approach. In this world view all preventive diplomatic action taken *must be collective in nature and selfish national interests have no place in this concept* (emphasis added).Therefore it is obvious that any definition of preventive diplomacy must have at its core the concept of universality and global significance. This view has in its support the fact that the world itself has become a "small village." The development of swift and comprehensive telecommunications has made light of frontiers and even universal problems such as pollution, climate change and changing demographics do not respect land or maritime frontiers.[10] As the economies of various countries in the world have become interlinked, world financial systems and stock markets do not respect national frontiers. Thus it is important that the approach adopted must be universally accepted and as broad-based as possible.

The focus of preventive diplomacy is not on solving *all* (emphasis added) of the humanitarian, political, or environmental problems of the world. That would be a task beyond the capacity of any organisation, including the UN, to fulfil. Instead, it is a specific response to a situation that is likely to result in violence between states or intra-state groups and is unlikely to be solved by local or national actors. Preventive diplomacy is not able to prevent every conflict, nor is it helpful in all situations. It is only one of the many tools, many options used by the international community to make peace a reality. Preventive diplomacy presents a range of policy options that hold great potential, but is at the moment a fairly underdeveloped mechanism.[11]

While definitions of what constitutes preventive diplomacy may vary however what is important is the fact that they should not be seen as being in contradiction to accepted international law. In international law sometimes a distinction is made between legal disputes and political disputes. This distinction arises from the attitude of the parties to a dispute. No state is likely to put at risk its vital interests or honour by accepting a method of settlement that takes into account only legal considerations. This difference is important for those practising preventive diplomacy, for they may not like to interfere or intervene when a conflict is of a legal nature. It is quite well understood that legal issues must be settled using legal mechanisms only, such as the application of arbitration and judicial procedures such as a reference to the International Court of Justice. Political disputes on the other hand, can be settled by a procedure that takes into account political imperatives and can use the options of negotiation, enquiry, good offices, mediation and conciliation. Sometimes the distinction is rather blurred and it is here that good sense of the practitioners of preventive diplomacy must prevail. Not all issues are as clear-cut and ever so obvious! Sometimes exercising positive discretion under the circumstances might be the right thing to do.

As far as international law is concerned, the UN Charter itself recognises the validity of this approach. The approach in the earlier stages was that the use of the option of using force to settle international disputes must be wholly discouraged. The UN Charter therefore reflects this sense and sentiment of the international community. The UN Charter under Article 2(4) states quite clearly that "all members shall refrain in their international relations from the threat or *use of force* against the territorial integrity or political independence of any state ..." As is obvious the key word here is *the use of force* (emphasis added). What the framers of the UN Charter had in mind was that, generally speaking, what we mean by the use of force refers to transnational or trans-boundary use of military threats. Before the threat or the use of force comes into play the opportunity for preventive diplomacy becomes available. However the framers of the UN Charter were not idealists. They had seen what happened in the case of the League of Nations earlier and what followed in the Second World War and therefore they were of the opinion that the *use of force could be authorised in certain circumstances* (emphasis added).

The first exception to the general rule was in the case of self-defence. Article 51 of the UN Charter embodies the right to use force in self-defence. It states as follows:

> Nothing in the present Charter shall impair the inherent right of individual or collective self-defence if an armed attack occurs against a Member of the United Nations, until the Security Council has taken measures necessary to maintain international peace and security. Measures taken by Members in the exercise of this right of self-defence shall be immediately reported to the Security Council and shall not in any way affect the authority and responsibility of the Security Council under the present Charter to take at any time such action as it deems necessary in order to maintain or restore international peace and security.

There are several key features to the Article 51 which contains the right of self-defence.

Firstly, it is a unilateral right. A state requires no approval from any external body to initiate self-defence measures. Secondly, Article 51 allows a state not only to defend itself completely on its own, but also to join others, such as partners in security alliances, in collectively repelling an armed attack launched by another state or a group of states. Thirdly, those who drafted the UN Charter at first contemplated that the right of self-defence would be an interim response. In their view states would be entitled to use force only until such time as the collective security machinery had responded satisfactorily to the initiation of hostilities. Fourthly, and most important of all, the right of self-defence recognised in the UN Charter is limited to situations in which an "armed attack" has occurred.

At the time the Charter was being negotiated the states involved in the negotiations and their personnel had only the experience of the First and Second World Wars before them. At that point in time the concept of non-state actors in conflict situations was unknown, nor were they familiar with guerrilla or terrorist activities. It is for this reason that there is emphasis in the UN Charter on "armed attack" situations. As could be expected there is no reference to terrorism or to non-state actors.

The second key feature was that states could utilise was the concept of collective security. Under the Charter, the United Nations Security Council is assigned the "primary responsibility for the maintenance of international peace and security." The Security Council, as presently constituted, comprises fifteen states: the five Great Powers that prevailed in the Second World War—the United States, the United Kingdom, France, Russia, and China and are permanent members (P-5)—as well as ten other states elected to serve on the Council for a two-year term. Acting pursuant to its authority under Chapter VII of the Charter, the Security Council is empowered to "determine the existence of any threat to the peace, breach of the peace, or act of aggression." In such circumstances, the Security Council "shall ... decide what measures shall be taken in accordance with Articles 41 and 42, to maintain or restore international peace and security." Measures available under Article 41 are those "not involving the use of armed force" to give effect to the Security Council's decisions. In addition, Article 42 of the Charter empowers the Security Council to "take such action by air, sea, or land forces as may be necessary to maintain or restore international peace and security. Such action may include demonstrations, blockade, and other operations by air, sea, or land forces of members of the United Nations." All members of the United Nations have "agree[d] to accept and carry out the decisions of the Security Council in accordance with the present Charter."

In view of the capacity of any of the five Permanent Members (P-5) of the Security Council to veto a proposed resolution authorising the use of force, means *that collective security measures are available only when there is unanimity among the Permanent Members in favour of such measures.* (Emphasis added). Secondly, in contrast to the right of self-defence, the prior commission of an armed attack is not a prerequisite to the exercise of force under Security Council authority. Rather, the Security Council may authorise measures, including the use of force, merely in the face of "threats" to international peace and security, including threats that may not yet be imminent. The Security Council, moreover, has largely unfettered power to determine what events and developments constitute such a threat. However the UN system is as much a product of the "great power" syndrome as were earlier international bodies. Its ability to act is a product of great power consensus, as otherwise it is a body that is often deadlocked.

In the international system one of the fundamental objectives, and as also envisaged in the UN Charter itself, is the concept *of the peaceful settlement of disputes.* This is referred to in Article 1 [1] of the UN Charter and is more explicitly stated in Article 2 [3]; which provides that *all members* "shall settle their international disputes by peaceful means in such a manner that international peace and security and justice are not endangered. This assertion becomes even more comprehensive in Article 33 [1]. Thus, as we can see, although collective security is one of the fundamental principles on which the international system was built, yet its pitfalls are quite evident.

While considering the concept of preventive diplomacy we must also recognise that it has obvious limitations. The first limitation is that there is a yawning gap between reality and rhetoric. Most nation states guard their sovereign rights with a great deal of zeal. This sentiment is also reflected in the UN Charter. In this respect Article 2 [7] is quite specific. It states as follows:

> Nothing contained in the present Charter shall authorise the UN to intervene in matters which are essentially in the domestic jurisdiction of any state.

This sentiment also gained widespread acceptance, as after the Second World War a large number of former colonies gained their independence. Having just achieved their hard won independence they did not wish to give any pretext to their former colonial masters to intervene in their internal affairs. This was an article of faith for many newly independent states. Therefore the difficulty that arose was: How to define a situation that was ripe for intervention? The international community was faced in the past with the vexed problem of apartheid. Was it an internal matter? This presented not only an issue, but also the larger question: When does it become an issue of such importance whose time has come for the international community to take over? Who should decide the timing? No clear answers are available. Not unnaturally, this was bound to take time for it is not easy for the international community to come to any conclusion at a speed that would not only make the intervention effective, but also successful.

On the other hand, most states even if they are the affected party would be loath to encourage any intervention no matter however benign it is. For these states the justification is provided by the UN Charter itself. The UN Charter does not recognise or refer to a "right" for humanitarian intervention, either for the individual state or for the international community. Many subsequent treaties, resolutions and statements have reaffirmed this view. For example Article 53/64 of the Vienna Convention on the Law of Treaties (1969) states that this particular provision is jus cogens and therefore accepted by the international community as a principle from which no derogation is permissible. Similarly the UN General Assembly Resolution 2131 of 1965 affirmed the Assembly's opposition to all forms of intervention for "any reason whatsoever." The same resolution also declared that "armed intervention is synonymous with aggression." Similarly Clause IV of the Helsinki Accords also recognises the same principle. Both the UN Charter and international law recognise the inviolability of the state and outlaw the use of force.[12]

Secondly, any intervention is very difficult to maintain over the long term period. Most nation states are not keen for over-extended periods of deployment, for most are strictly monitored by their respective finance and personnel departments. Unless the cause has some bearing on national interests and there is some element of gain involved, whether it is political or economic or even strategic, very few countries would sustain a long-term involvement. Any intervention, even preventive, is not an inexpensive option. It requires a strong financial commitment and given that most states are not in robust economic health, few would like to make an open-ended commitment either financially or in terms of their personnel. In this context the then UN Secretary-General Boutros-Ghali identified two problems. The first (problem) is the difficulty of finding senior persons who have the diplomatic skills and who are willing to serve for a while as a special representative or special envoy of the Secretary-General. As a result of the streamlining of the senior levels of the Secretariat, the extra capacity that was there in earlier years no longer exists.[13] Although through a system of instituting special envoys some achievement is possible on a visiting basis, their capacity would be greatly enhanced if continuity could be assured by the presence on the ground of small support missions on a full-time basis. However, even these activities would have to be financed and therefore it would be necessary to include in the regular budget a contingency provision, which might be in the range of say $25 million per biennium, for such activities. The second option would be to enlarge the existing provision for unseen and extraordinary activities and to make it available for all preventive and peacemaking activities, not just those related to international peace and security.[14]

One of the most obvious problems in pursuing a programme of strengthened preventive diplomacy at the United Nations is the general financial crisis. As of March 1996, member states owed the United Nations $3.2 billion in overdue contributions. Of this, the US owed approximately $1.6 billion for past debts and current obligations. The financial crisis is so severe that the UN may have to temporarily close its doors. It is crucial that UN preventive diplomacy be adequately and independently funded; to achieve this, member states must promptly pay all dues to the UN. Ample funds should be provided for preventive diplomacy through the UN System. Former Secretary-General Boutros-Ghali's above suggestions are one way that this could be accomplished. Member states should take an even more active role in developing the concept of preventive diplomacy through additional voluntary contributions earmarked for preventive diplomacy programmes.[15]

Take for example the financial resources spent by the US in Iraq. A *New York Times* study published in August 2004 showed that the US$ 144 billion already then spent in Iraq (and that figure is now closer to $400 billion!) by the US could have paid for, among other things, the more or less complete safeguarding of US ports, airports and airliners ($34 billion); the security from theft of the world's stock of weapons-grade nuclear materials and the deactivation of warheads (another $34 billion); the complete rebuilding of Afghanistan, including drug crop conversion ($20 billion); the recruitment to the military of another 65,000 US troops, if anyone thought this a good idea ($40 billion); plus another $10 billion in development assistance to deserving underdeveloped countries which would have helped alleviate poverty and perhaps prevent unwanted conflict.[16]

It is not only additional financial resources that are needed for conflict prevention and resolution, but a more intelligent application of the resources already being spent, not least on the armed forces themselves. A critical resource problem constantly facing planners is the availability of deployable military assets of the necessary quality for peacekeeping, peace enforcement and peace building tasks. A major part of the problem in the developed world is the lingering on of Cold War configurations in force structures. Though it is insidious yet for example, to single out any single country when the problem is so endemic. In Germany, of the 250,000 men and women currently in uniform, only some 10,000 are deployable at any given time on international peace operation tasks. One recent broader estimate is that of the 2.5 million personnel nominally under arms in Europe, at most 3 per cent are deployable.[17] Thus it is very important to discuss in advance as to who will take the lead politically, who will decide how many troops are required for deployment, who will take command of the troops and even if sufficient financial resources are available and have been committed, how are these to be deployed? The question of logistics is very important.

At the same time interventions are hardly likely to be successful if the root causes are not properly tackled. Most such issues require a certain amount of attention to detail. Therefore what actually happens is that nation states wary of such long-term involvement often take the easiest route out and that is to do nothing. It is often said that "the greatest cause of failure has been intervener fatigue and premature satisfaction with the results."[18]

One of the major pitfalls and a major limitation for preventive diplomacy is the question of political will. It is common for most states to base their foreign policy on perceived national interest. This includes ensuring the safety and security of its territory, the well-being of its people and to be able to meet the potential threats of its likely adversaries. The fundamental point in almost all areas of public policy is that unless the relevant decision-makers, both at the national or international level, decide on a line of action, nothing tangible is likely to happen. At the end of the day no matter if the concepts are right, if the analysis is right and all the resources and capacity required are available, yet it is very unlikely if any action taken can succeed without the consent of the great powers. Of course, what has to be understood is the fact that there does exist, a lack of political will. Simply leaving it at that will not move matters forward. However what also has to be recognised is how to mobilise it, recognising and squarely deal with all the institutional dynamics and personalities and interests involved. No one argument can fit all and therefore it would have to be suitably amended to meet the exigencies of the day. And that requires a combination of good institutional structures and good arguments.[19] Some of the "good" arguments in favour of exercising the necessary political will are:

- The financial aspect. There is no doubt that preventive action taken well in time is far cheaper financially than responding to events after they have taken place whether through military action, humanitarian relief assistance, reconstruction costs or deployment of post-conflict troops for peacekeeping duties. A recent survey by the World Bank has estimated that the average cost of a civil war is equivalent to more than 30 years of GDP growth of a medium-sized developing country.[20]
- The national interest. The world today is an inter-dependent one and therefore even if conflicts are taking place far away, the risks are not that far away. The world is becoming much "smaller" with the advent of instant media which flashes news from one corner of the world to the other in just a few seconds. No state can remain immune from its effects and influence. Thus conflicts such as terrorism, health pandemics and refugee outflows and economic and financial interdependence cannot be dealt with in isolation.

- Domestic political considerations. Sometimes events that take place outside the territorial jurisdiction of a state have a bearing on its domestic political situation. For example, a religious conflict presents peculiar difficulties since co-religionists may be facing extreme pressure. The Bush Administration's desire for continued support from its right-wing Christian constituents certainly was an important element in its wholly desirable commitment to peace processes in Sudan.
- The moral argument and idealism. It is often said that idealism has no place in the making of foreign policy. But the argument is not that idealism should be a stand-alone factor, but that the costs of always following an inward looking policy maybe that much higher. Therefore the most effective foreign policy for any country, whatever its weight, is one that balances realism and idealism—that in effect makes idealism realistic.[21] But if idealism has its limits, the substitute is not a unidimensional brand of foreign policy realism either. A foreign policy that is founded only on hard-headed realism is a policy that can all too readily descend into cynical indifference, with results that may not be palatable later. Successful foreign policy options that are exercised have of necessity to reflect domestic opinion and must be based on a principled and judicious mixture of both idealism and realism.

An important element in that mix is a willingness to accept the principle of "the responsibility to protect" (R2P), but which must not contain "hidden" agendas. The principle of "R2P" means that while the primary responsibility to protect its own people vests entirely with the government concerned, yet in extreme circumstances when it is unable to do so, such responsibility should then vest with the international community. This concept was recognised within the international community with the UN General Assembly endorsing it in 2005. This was also unanimously affirmed by the UN Security Council by Resolution 1694 passed in 2006 and again in 2009 under Resolution 1894 which was also passed without any opposition. However this does not mean that this gives the great powers the licence to undertake a "regime change." Quite often newly independent states have genuine worries that this concept of "R2P" is nothing but another attempt to interfere in the internal affairs of nation states. Therefore it is imperative that some principles be evolved or guidelines instituted that would guide intervention in the name of "R2P." In any case such intervention cannot be selective. Therefore crimes such as terrorism, weapons proliferation, drug and people trafficking, the spread of health pandemics and other global risks should be clearly identified and listed before action is initiated. Such action must always be for the good of common humanity and address the distress and agony of our fellow human beings and not for political, economic or strategic gain. With the obligation for "R2P" also goes hand in hand the obligation to rebuild. It is not simply a question of intervention, whether it is diplomatic or with the use of force, but there is the larger question of rebuilding the institutions, civil society and organs of governance. Otherwise an intervention would only be counterproductive with no change in the situation and it may come to be seen as only a "regime change." If nothing else changes except the regime then the effort is hardly worth it.

Thus once the arguments are successfully presented it should be possible to urge states to take action when it is urgently required. This is where the concept of preventive diplomacy has its greatest value for it does present a low cost option before things really get out of hand. If by preventive diplomacy a crisis that is brewing can be controlled at the initial stages or a crisis that has already erupted can be prevented from spreading further, no matter how we define preventive diplomacy it would be a substantive gain for common humanity. Finally as the present UN Secretary-General put it in his report on preventive diplomacy:

> While preventive diplomacy has grown and evolved significantly, it is neither easy nor straightforward nor inevitably successful. It continues to face great obstacles and long odds, with success often hostage to multiple factors, one of the most critical of which is the will of the parties. If the parties do not want peace or are unwilling to compromise, it is extraordinarily difficult, especially for outsiders, to persuade them otherwise. In such cases, the linkage between preventive diplomacy and the power to produce incentives and disincentives can be critical to convince key actors, with due respect for their sovereignty, that there is value in choosing dialogue over violence and, if necessary, to accept external assistance to that end.

CHAPTER TWO

SOME BASIC PRINCIPLES OR GUIDELINES FOR PREVENTIVE DIPLOMACY

In the interdependent world that we live in today it is necessary that international disputes and conflicts be settled peacefully, if international peace and security are to be maintained. The UN Charter recognises this aspect when it categorically affirms under Article 2, paragraph 5 that:

> All member states shall give the United Nations every assistance in any action it takes in accordance with the present Charter and shall refrain from giving assistance to any state against which the UN is taking preventive or enforcement action.

As the membership of the UN, as at present, is nearly universal in nature it therefore follows that the obligation to settle all disputes peacefully has international sanction. Recent judicial pronouncements are also of the same view.[1] Further under Article 33, paragraph 1, the UN Charter also specifies the methods which states might wish to use to settle their disputes peacefully. Nevertheless, before such principles or guidelines are examined it is also important to first of all diagnose the cause of the conflict, whether it be handled regionally or at the international level and what the response of the international community should be. In this respect there is the widespread belief that the sooner a problem is attended to the lesser the chances of it getting out of hand and that it would be also very cost-effective. Therefore the stress has in recent times been on finding the best method of instituting an early warning system.

In the past one of the major problems faced by the UN system was the lack of authentic information. Sometimes there is too much information, given the fact that the world is now undergoing a media revolution. In these days of instant communications, there is the need within the UN system to be able to collate all the information flowing in, to study it and to be able to recommend action on it. Thus cooperation within the various agencies of the UN is very important. Recently, the present UN Secretary-General reported that:

> Cooperation within the United Nations on early warning has improved. Specialised parts of the system such as the Office of the United Nations High Commissioner for Human Rights (OHCHR) and the Office of the Special Adviser for the Prevention of Genocide and Mass Atrocities are playing a key role in filtering information and drawing attention to such dangerous indicators as patterns of human rights violations or hate speech, which might otherwise escape detection. Similarly, closer cooperation between the United Nations and regional organizations such as the African Union and ECOWAS, both of which operate early warning systems, has ensured more and better data.

However, the quality of the inferences drawn still varies and there is the need for better coordination. The UN system is unable to adequately anticipate or identify "threshold moments when states to a conflict decide, or feel compelled, to use an escalation of violence to achieve their objectives." The better the diagnosis and analysis of the motives and calculations of states, the better the preventive response can be worked out. It is often said that proximity to any situation combined with local knowledge and regular local contact vastly improves any analysis of the impending crisis. It is noticeable that the United Nations has begun to work more closely with civil society members, politicians, and members of the business community, influential academic institutions and think tanks on the ground. Women's groups in particular play an important role in early warning. It is important that these activities be increased for they play an important role in helping shape a proper response.

No matter how early the information is received or how accurate it is, the real test is whether it leads to early action. As the UN Secretary-General has pointed out, "the difference between a successful engagement and one that is likely to fail can often be measured in the time that has lapsed between the first warning signs of a problem and the first steps taken to address it. This warning-to-action continuum is the challenge the international community can find hardest to meet. However, even if the actions taken are small, for example a statement of concern by the Security Council, the deployment of a fact-finding mission or a well-timed demarche by the Secretary-General, these can have a more important effect on the calculations of states than a larger but more slowly developed response.

This is true especially when these actions clearly signal a sustained focus by the international community." The key therefore is whether despite all the information available of impending conflict, what if any action was taken. Thus, having received all the information, what are the methods available for taking resolute action?

The UN Charter itself specifies under Article 33, paragraph 1 the methods that are available. It must be emphasised that the UN Charter lays heavy responsibility on finding "peaceful" methods for solving disputes. The options listed are: negotiation, enquiry, mediation, conciliation, arbitration, judicial settlement, resort to regional agencies or arrangements, or other peaceful means of their own choice. The UN Secretary-General also has the option of offering his "good offices" and a range of expertise in settlement dispute processes. Finally, if all else fails states can take recourse to the UN Security Council and the General Assembly. Let us examine each one of these methods and see if they are really successful in solving disputes.

It is said that negotiations are the simplest form of settlement of disputes for the parties to the dispute are themselves directly involved. This is in contrast to other methods where other parties not directly involved might at some stage become parties to the settlement of the dispute. In its very basic form negotiations are a continuing form of dialogue between the parties concerned and even when complicated cases are involved the main aim is to narrow differences so that a reasonable settlement is possible that is acceptable to both sides. The success or otherwise of the negotiations depends upon how wide the gap is between the two parties. It also depends upon their respective diplomatic skill as also the relative power that can be exercised. It is not always the case that negotiations have failed if the two parties are not able to come to an agreement. Even if the gap is narrowed to a considerable extent, negotiations cannot be said to be a failure. The key for success is that negotiations should not be broken off.

The main channels for negotiations are the Diplomatic Missions of the two parties in their respective capitals and these channels can be supplemented by messages and personal meetings between the officials and leading political personalities of the two countries. Often other channels are also used such as individuals having no governmental positions, party leaders, newspaper editors or businessmen having contacts, on the condition that the two parties concerned accept such roles.

There is no doubt that negotiations have a much wider role to play, but contemporary negotiations are also very much more complicated than in the past. This is the aspect of multilateralism, an aspect that now looms large in the handling of international relations. Meetings are now frequently held in multinational forums where decisions are taken and where sometimes several states also participate in the negotiations leading to a possible settlement. However not all were convinced that this was an appropriate method of negotiation. As the then UN Secretary-General Dag Hammarskjold said, "they have introduced a new instrument of negotiation, that of conference diplomacy. This instrument has many advantages. [...] But it has, also, weaknesses. There is the temptation to play to the gallery at the expense of solid construction. And there is the risk that positions once taken publicly, become frozen making a compromise more difficult."[2] At the same time the International Court of Justice (ICJ) in its judicial pronouncements emphasised the importance of negotiations and in fact the UN Law of the Sea places an obligation on all states to settle all disputes peacefully and through negotiations.

Another method is that of Enquiry. Strictly speaking an enquiry is not a method of settlement of disputes. An enquiry imposes no duty on the parties to a dispute to settle and there is no guarantee that a conflict will be settled, but what it does do is to bring the facts of the case out into the open. With the clarification of facts thus provided, it becomes that much easier for the parties to conduct negotiations. In his report to the UN Security Council the UN Secretary-General pointed out that this method had been particularly helpful. He said, "member States faced with situations of politically sensitive crimes, violent incidents or alleged grave human rights violations have increasingly turned to the Organisation to conduct impartial inquiries. Some of these have been mandated by the Security Council or by the Human Rights Council, while others have been established by the Secretary-General. The entities created are as diverse as the situations and requests they respond to. Though not part of the traditional conflict prevention toolkit, these mechanisms have, in recent years, been effectively leveraged to support preventive diplomacy efforts, helping to shift the calculations of the parties, defuse tensions and build confidence. For instance, a joint fact-finding inquiry carried out with ECOWAS into the deaths of Ghanaian migrants found in the Gambia in 2007 was seen as helpful in rebuilding relations between the two countries. Other examples include the United Nations-backed International Commission against Impunity in Guatemala, created in 2007 to help the country to investigate and dismantle clandestine criminal networks; the Commission of Inquiry to investigate the events of September 28, 2009 in Conakry; and the Panel of Inquiry on the Gaza flotilla incident of May 31, 2010."[3]

Mediation is a very important method for peacefully settling disputes. The role of the mediator was well expressed in Article 4 of the Hague Convention on the Pacific Settlement of Disputes 1899. The article states as follows: "reconciling opposing claims and appeasing the feeling of resentment which may have arisen between the states at variance." Thus his role begins when there is agreement between the states and the mediator on the role that is envisaged for him. A mediator may represent one or two or more states, but he must be acceptable to all. While he can offer suggestions for facilitating a settlement, parties to the dispute need not accept his suggestions nor are they bound by them. However there are some essential qualities that a mediator must possess. These are: (1) Moderation. A mediator must not prevaricate in telling one party the position of the other, but should try to soften the demands to facilitate a settlement. (2) Perseverance. Many disputes cannot be solved in a hurry and therefore call for extraordinary patience and perseverance. (3) Preparation and Knowledge. A mediator must have detailed knowledge of the subject under dispute as well as its history and background. If he can understand the ethos and reasons why this dispute arose in the first place and why it is so important for either of the parties, then his task becomes that much easier. A mediator should also try and fathom a solution and this calls for ingenuity and imagination on his part. (4) It goes without saying that a mediator must exercise absolute impartiality and independence from the parties to the dispute.

In the United Nations system the Department of Political Affairs has taken the lead role in providing a platform for parties to a dispute to utilise its services for achieving a settlement. The Department was strengthened over the past three years to play its lead role in preventive diplomacy within the United Nations system more effectively. It has enhanced its analytical capacities, its technical expertise in key areas such as electoral assistance, its partnerships and its ability to learn lessons, distil best practices and facilitate system-wide responses. As a result, it is becoming better geared towards rapid response, and through its Mediation Support Unit it can offer mediation initiatives worldwide. Its standby team of mediation experts is able to deploy within 72 hours to assist negotiators on peace process design, security arrangements, in constitution-making, gender issues, power-sharing and wealth-sharing. A dedicated mechanism, supported by voluntary contributions, provides more flexible financing for rapid response.[4]

Another method is conciliation. Conciliation as a means of settlement of disputes of any nature according to which a commission set up by the parties to the dispute, either on a permanent or an ad hoc basis to deal with the disputes, proceeds to inquire into the facts underlying the dispute and possibly after discussions with the parties concerned issues a formal, but not binding proposal, for consideration of the parties concerned as a solution for the dispute.[5] Conciliation is to be distinguished from mediation in that it involves an inquiry and an investigation into the facts by the conciliators. By contrast a mediator has no such facility. Further the method of conciliation is to be distinguished from an Enquiry in that in addition to elucidating facts a conciliator goes forward to make positive proposals for a solution. Finally, the method of conciliation is to be distinguished from a judicial proceeding in that its recommendations do not have any binding validity. It leaves unchallenged the sovereign rights of the parties to a dispute who have no obligation to accept its verdict. The parties to a dispute also do not lose their position nor do they lose their inherent rights. It must be pointed out however that the method of conciliation is given high importance in the UN Law of the Sea.

One of the useful methods for settling disputes has been the utilising of the offer of "good offices" mainly from international organisations as also from distinguished individuals. Good offices means the action taken by a third party to bring about or initiate negotiations between the parties concerned, but without participation in the actual negotiations. As an inducement the offer of "good offices" may include the giving of advice or even offering solutions but it certainly does not include any obligation of either of the two parties to a dispute to accept such advice or solutions.

The offer of "good offices" has been in vogue particularly in the UN system. This stems largely from the belief that the UN Secretary-General being a neutral personality, states may utilise his services for facilitating a solution. The present UN Secretary-General sees his role as follows:

> My mandate for conflict prevention originates in Article 99 of the Charter, which provides that the Secretary-General may bring to the attention of the Security Council any matter which, in his opinion, may threaten the maintenance of international peace and security. Successive Secretaries-General have used their good offices to help parties find

> solutions to problems at the earliest possible stage. The effectiveness of the good offices is often a function of how much political space the Secretary-General has in which to act. In my own experience, the most difficult scenario is when international interest is strong but conflicted, because the parties know that there is no unity of vision. As a custodian of the Charter, I also have the duty to speak out in certain situations, an obligation which may or may not enhance mediation efforts. At times, public advocacy in full view of the media is necessary; more often, however, good offices are deployed behind the scenes. Irrespective of the approach, the key is to practice diplomacy that is as determined as it is flexible.[6]

Apart from offering his "good offices" the UN Secretary-General also has been utilising the concept of sending "special envoys" to the parties concerned in order to help them arrive at solutions and facilitate agreement. These envoys have been able to defuse tension, resolve problems in the context of border disputes and territorial questions, help in regional conflicts, provide expertise in constitutional and electoral issues, offer suggestions to facilitate regional peace talks and most important of all, pull back from the brink regional conflicts that threatened to go out of hand. This aspect of the UN Secretary-General's work was explained by him as follows:

> For example, in the autumn of 2008, I appointed former Nigerian President, General Olusegun Obasanjo, as Special Envoy for the Great Lakes in the context of growing tension and a widespread fear that the Democratic Republic of the Congo would again become the theatre of regional war. With

backstopping from Headquarters and in close consultation with the United Nations peacekeeping operation on the ground, the Special Envoy engaged in intense shuttle diplomacy in search of a negotiated peace in the eastern Democratic Republic of the Congo. Collaborating with the International Conference on the Great Lakes Region, these efforts resulted, within just a few weeks, in complex peace talks under United Nations auspices, made possible through the rapid deployment of a mediation support team, together with associated logistics, translation services and conference and travel support. By March 2009, the talks had led to a set of agreements foreseeing the demobilisation and disarmament of rebel groups and measures to address their underlying grievances. With ongoing engagement by the Special Envoy to monitor progress, the bulk of the commitments were implemented within less than a year. In late 2009, Presidents Kagame and Kabila met for the first time in many years, and shortly thereafter Rwanda and the Democratic Republic of the Congo resumed formal diplomatic relations. While the situation in the eastern Democratic Republic of the Congo remains serious in terms of generalised insecurity and humanitarian suffering, renewed regional war was averted. In other instances, the Organisation has played a supportive role. In January 2008, for example, amid post election violence in Kenya, the African Union mandated a process chaired by former Secretary-General Kofi Annan, to avert further deterioration into a civil war along ethnic lines. This effort was strongly supported by the United Nations country team on the ground and staff sent from the Department of Political Affairs, drawing strategically on expert advice from the Department's Electoral Assistance Division and other actors. The power-sharing agreement reached not only served to avert conflict but also provided the basis for a new constitution.[7]

Finally if all other methods fail there is always the UN Security Council and the UN General Assembly that can be approached. It would be useful to examine what role the Security Council can play and whether it is an effective mechanism for solving disputes between nation states. Can it for example play the role of preventing conflict even at the incipient stages? Can it conduct effective preventive diplomacy?

The Security Council is the main organ of the United Nations that it tasked with the maintenance of peace and security in the world. To a large degree the reputation of the UN system is dependent on the effectiveness and activity of the Security Council. The composition, functions and procedures of the Security Council are dealt with under Chapter V, Articles 23 to 32 of the UN Charter. An important aspect of its functioning is the fact that the UNSC is in permanent session and can be summoned for a session within hours. The powers of the Council are fairly substantial and wide and under Article 24 members of the UN agree that the council has the primary responsibility for the maintenance of international peace and security. They also agree that the UNSC carries out its functions on their behalf and furthermore under Article 25 they accept in advance to carry out its directions.

In practice however the UNSC has obvious limitations. The most important one is that where the interests of the great powers are concerned, it becomes almost paralysed. This is not only because the great powers exercise the veto when their own interests are involved, but very often do not let any resolution pass that might affect their own allies no matter how odious their behaviour. For years on end the US has not allowed any resolution to pass that censures Israel, even if it is clearly shown that Israel has been the aggressor. Similarly, during the days of the cold war, the former Soviet Union would regularly veto any resolution that was even mildly critical of its actions. The key issue is that the Security Council has no armed forces of its own and is thus dependent on contributions by member states. Very often even if states are supportive of or even critical of a developing situation they seem to be quite satisfied by passing resolutions, but are extremely loath to take any military action or even offer troops for action unless their own interests are affected. And if the offending state is a major power or even a nuclear weapons power, then there is absolutely no inclination to use force to enforce UN resolutions. At best what might be attempted is a form of economic sanctions. And these are sometimes also only on paper.

In the past, the UNSC concentrated largely on dealing with conflicts and other emergent situations *only after the event had occurred* (emphasis added). However in recent years there has been a change in that the UNSC has made a push for greater commitment and flexibility in addressing emerging threats before they are placed on the UNSC's formal agenda. For example, since early 2008, the Council has held "informal interactive dialogues" on a range of situations, which are intended to promote a more proactive approach to preventive diplomacy. It has requested the Department of Political Affairs to deliver monthly "horizon scanning" briefings that focus on current and emerging conflicts. The present Secretary-General has been holding "informal monthly luncheons with the Security Council to raise many items that are not on any formal agenda."[8] Since 2007, the thematic item "peace and security in Africa" has served to address a variety of country-specific issues in formal meetings, including situations not officially on the Security Council's agenda. The question that however still remains unanswered is: When should the Security Council become involved and at what stage? This is a question that remains in the public domain for there is no definitive answer. At times, the Security Council may decide for good reasons to keep its decision in reserve, in order to leave sufficient space for quiet or preventive diplomacy. In other instances, highly visible and decisive action by the Security Council, such as missions to the field, initiatives by its President and press communiqués, may open enough political space for prevention which otherwise would not have existed. When the Security Council forms a common view for addressing a situation of concern, then often its decision becomes most effective. For example, the present Secretary-General has reported that "in the case of Guinea's constitutional crisis in 2009 and 2010 and the Southern Sudan 2011 independence referendum, it (the UNSC) has proven its effectiveness in generating political momentum and engaging with key interlocutors in pursuit of a common strategy." The key issue for its effectiveness is the common will of its members.

Another organ of the UN system which can play an effective role is the General Assembly. Under Articles 10 and 11 of the UN Charter the General Assembly has a wide charter to consider conflict prevention in all aspects. The General Assembly provides a valuable platform from which participating states can interact with each other. Its wide and nearly universal membership gives it this unique opportunity. On June 22, 2011 the General Assembly adopted by consensus a resolution that emphasised the strengthening of the role of mediation in the peaceful settlement of disputes and conflict prevention. This resolution[9] is a groundbreaking development that positions the Assembly as a setter of standards for mediation and provides a broad framework for productive collaboration with member states and regional organisations. However what are the practical consequences of an assembly that only debates, tables resolutions and also eventually votes, but it cannot bind any state to its resolutions? No matter how large are the majorities of the vote, it cannot carry them out for its resolutions are only recommendatory in nature. In a very strict interpretation therefore the General Assembly lacks authority, but it must be pointed out that in this day of rapid communications even these resolutions do resonate with the authorities of any state and hence its importance in preventing conflict.

Another fairly effective method is to use the office of the UN Secretary-General for preventive diplomacy. Successive Secretaries-General have used their good offices to help parties find solutions to problems at the earliest possible stage. The effectiveness of the good offices depends upon how much political space the Secretary-General has in which to act and the personality of the holder of this office. Very often if relations between the great powers are poor then there is little scope for the Secretary-General to play a role. Or conversely, if they are good then they may not need his services at all. It is only when relations are in the "grey" area that his role assumes importance. As the present Secretary-General has said, "In my own experience, the most difficult scenario is when international interest is strong, but conflicted, because the parties know that there is no unity of vision. As a custodian of the Charter, I also have the duty to speak out in certain situations, an obligation which may or may not enhance mediation efforts."[10] However, under the UN Charter the Secretary-General is given the right under Article 99 to bring any threatening matter to the notice of the UN Security Council. This article gives him the scope, if he wishes to utilise it, to play an independent political role rather than just an administrator of an international organisation. It is here that the question of the personality of the incumbent comes into play. If the Secretary-General is a talented and a thrusting person he can with sufficient zeal and resourcefulness assume a sharper and a more significant international role. On the other hand if the personality of the incumbent is passive and submissive then not much can be expected of the office of the Secretary-General. He at best would only swim along with the current tide. The reality is that a powerful Secretary-General is rarely welcome and therefore unusual.Nevertheless the incumbent of the office of the UN Secretary-General must possess credibility, inspire trust and confidence, be discreet and above all reflect transparency, impartiality and confidentiality. He must give the impression that even the most intractable problems are soluble. It is a given that it is the member states that determine how much leeway a Secretary-General should be allowed and customarily that leeway has not been large. In this the UN, as an international organisation, basically reflects the situation that prevails in that the UN is an organisation consisting of sovereign states and therefore it has to reflect their will.

Nevertheless a Secretary-General can be innovative. The decision to send personal envoys to trouble spots or post UN special representatives or to constitute a "peace building" commission, are important such examples. The peace building commission is an intergovernmental advisory body of the Security Council and the General Assembly. Its main purpose was to ensure a sustained international attention to states that were emerging from a conflict situation. An important aspect was the attention that was paid to the reconstruction and institution-building efforts that were necessary for recovery from conflict. Six countries are currently on the commission's agenda: These are Burundi, the Central African Republic, Guinea, Guinea-Bissau, Liberia and Sierra Leone. Country-specific configurations of the commission have been established in each case, which could help to prevent relapse into violence.

While there are a range of methods available from which a suitable one that matches the need of the occasion can be found, the important aspect that should be kept in mind is that at the end of the day what is important is the will with which this action is implemented. Choosing a method of operation is only one half of the initiative, taking positive and sustained action is the other and perhaps more important part. Sometimes the choice that is made is beyond capacity, for it may be dictated by circumstances or by the great powers of the day. Nevertheless a choice once made should be seen through its entire implementation period or otherwise the solution may be worse than the disease.

There is, however, a need for an institutionalisation of the practice of preventive diplomacy. As noted by Michael Lund, "to get beyond the occasional ad hoc effort and individual success story, the question of which actors should play the roles on an ongoing basis and how they should relate to one another has to be faced. Some sort of system is needed that would allocate mutual expectations and responsibilities and assign various tasks of preventive diplomacy to one or more actors." It is important to note that any system should not be so inflexible as to further handicap the many actors, but should only provide the structure necessary to make the preventive action successful. This system should not be the singular responsibility of the UN Secretariat, but should be based on a multilateral system of burden-sharing. However, the role of the UN in any such system would be significant, for although the UN would not control the entire system, it would rest at its apex. Currently there are neither the resources nor the political will for the UN to meet its current responsibilities, much less the increased role it is being asked to play.

CHAPTER THREE

A STRATEGY FOR IMPLEMENTATION

When devising a strategy for implementation of preventive diplomacy it is important that two broad fundamental aspects be kept in mind. The first part of the strategy would include only non-coercive methods and non-military methods. The second part of the strategy would include the use of force and therefore the question that would arise is: when should force be used, how much should be used, who should authorise it and under what circumstances should it be used? The question of the use of force is a very important one for the entire international system has been built on the assumption that nation states are sovereign and that nothing should be done to violate their sovereignty. Even the UN recognises this proposition for under Article 2[7] of the UN Charter it was clearly stated that "nothing contained in the present charter shall authorise the UN to intervene in matters which are essentially within the domain of the domestic jurisdiction of the state." This aspect was further reinforced in Article 2[4] of the UN Charter which states that "all members shall refrain in their international relations from the threat or use of force against the territorial integrity or political independence of any state."

While the UN Charter supports non-interference in internal affairs of a state, it also provides an exception to this general rule. The principle of non-interference does not apply to peace-enforcement measures taken under Chapter VII of the UN Charter where there is a clause that allows the use of force. In such a case the principle of non-interference in domestic affairs of a state is not applicable. For example, UN sanctions were imposed on South Africa because apartheid, even though a domestic issue, was regarded as a threat to international peace and security. Intervention in Somalia was based on a similar interpretation. Numerous other Articles in the UN Charter, for example, Article 3 affirm that "everyone has the right to life, liberty and the security of person," and Article 55 commits the UN to "promote ... universal respect for, and observance of, human rights and fundamental freedoms." Similarly Article 56 pledges all members "to take joint and separate action" towards this end. Further affirmations of the inalienability of basic human rights are ensconced in the Genocide Convention, the Universal Declaration of Human Rights, and other International Covenants that make no distinction as to whether the offender is a foreigner or one's own government. Former UN Secretary-General, Kofi Annan made an important statement that:

> the [UN] Charter was issued in the name of the peoples, not the governments of the United Nations. ...The Charter protects the sovereignty of peoples. It was never meant as a licence for governments to trample on human rights and human dignity. Sovereignty implies responsibility, not just power.

Annan goes on to stress the legitimacy of interventions based on the Chapter VII provision for preserving international peace and security even when the locus of the conflict is intrastate. As an agonised Annan asked, "if humanitarian intervention is, indeed, an unacceptable assault on sovereignty, how then should we respond to a Rwanda, to a Srebrenica to gross and systematic violations of human rights?" This obvious qualification of the principle of absolute sovereignty has led to the belief that sovereignty is of the people and not that of a state. It is on this account that most humanitarian interventions have been justified. Similar duality pertains to the macro level of regional and international security. In fact, some important precedents have been set in the 1990s of the UN Security Council—authorised interventions abridging sovereignty such as with UNSC 688 (1991) that authorised a peacekeeping mission to protect the Kurds in Northern Iraq. Most cases, though, have been to protect refugees and for other humanitarian purposes and are not designed to be political in nature. Therefore while stressing the non-coercive and non-military aspects of intervention for the maintenance of international peace and security peace, it is not a foregone conclusion that state sovereignty must be protected on each and every occasion.

At the very outset it needs to be clarified that preventive diplomacy is not the panacea for all the ills affecting the international system and nor can it be applied in each and every case. It has to be selectively applied and it is not a question of one solution that fits all circumstances. Therefore different methods, differing solutions would have to be devised depending upon the circumstances of each case. As such the strategy devised in one case may not be the answer in another case. But before any strategy can be devised it is important to first study the case, determine what caused it or in other words look at the root causes of the conflict and only then determine the strategy to be followed. As the Carnegie Commission on Global Governance (1995) put it, "a comprehensive political strategy must first focus on the underlying political, social, economic and environment causes of conflict."[1] The further question that arises is: should it be dealt with at the regional level and left to regional organisations to devise a strategy or should it be elevated to the international level? And who should take such a decision?

The point at issue is that even after receiving all the early warnings and information about an impending crisis, states are still very reluctant to take action. The problem is not that there is no early warning, but that there is no early action. The reasons for not taking early action are not far to seek. Firstly, most states as a general tendency assess the stakes to be rather low. At such an initial stage of their development, such contingencies are simply not perceived to pose grave enough threats to a state's core national interests. Moreover, whether it will remain a low-level conflict, or escalate to a major crisis that would eventually involve the key strategic interests of a state or of the international community often remain problematical and are difficult to estimate at that early stage.

Secondly, no matter how efficient the forecast has been there will always be considerable skepticism and uncertainty and very likely there will be no unanimity of interpretation. It is not that prospective key trouble spots cannot be identified; rather the issue is in understanding such situations well enough to forecast which ones are likely to shatter peace and the time frame in which it happens. Estimates are never unanimous on how serious a situation will eventually become. No one can accurately surmise whether it would further escalate and how soon?

Thirdly, there is a dearth of trained political experts who can interpret the material received and relate it early symptoms and thereafter give a definitive interpretation. This is an art which is acquired after much political experience in the field and not something that is available in textbooks.

Fourthly, even where there is a relatively good early warning, policymakers, who are usually hard-headed bureaucrats, are often reluctant to take preventive action because they are inherently conservative in nature in their approach to issues. These policymakers, typically preoccupied with a battery of "other" problems that require urgent attention, often give only the barest attention to new, low-level crises that may never develop into serious concerns.[2]

Fifthly, and related to this is the fact that overloaded with other work an official tasked with interpretation of an early warning often puts it aside for it to be decided later. Given the large number of simmering crises and given the ever-growing limitation of resources, policymakers find it impractical to respond with preventive actions to all of them, a thinking that is reinforced by the general lack of knowledge regarding what efforts would be effective. Early warning of an equivocal, uncertain nature in such situations is insufficient for costly or risky responses.

Sixthly, sometimes reluctance to act in the face of early warning may not be because the warning is not taken seriously, but rather because decision makers are convinced that any involvement now would lead to even greater involvement later and that it would be better to abstain so that there is no involvement in this "nasty problem." This dilemma is particularly poignant for political leaders who must weigh incurring political costs now (in addition to the human and material costs that action entails) for benefits that will accrue downstream, if at all, with no guarantees that they would be given credit for preventing a disaster, that for the present appears to be a non-event. Thus, even in cases where the prospect of a catastrophe is taken seriously, there may be a lack of "political will" to take timely and effective action. Numerous observers have noted that governments often ignore an incipient crisis until it has escalated into a deadly struggle or a major catastrophe. All too often political leaders find it difficult to persuade their people to support potentially costly and risky operations before a disaster actually occurs (ibid). People generally tend to be guided by media reports. TV coverage and reports are not there unless the situation turns into large-scale violence, destruction and devastation and death. It is only then that they begin to take notice and it therefore follows that governments too begin to take notice only then!

Assuming that "action" is on the anvil, what are the non-coercive, non-military options and opportunities that are available? Generally speaking these are listed as (1) Conflict Prevention Efforts (2) Peace Keeping (3) Peace Making (4) Peace Enforcement and included in this is the aspect of "sanctions" and (5) Peace Building.

According to the UN handbook on "principles and guidelines" of peacekeeping, the definition of conflict prevention involves the application of structural or diplomatic measures to keep intra-state or interstate tensions and disputes from escalating into violent conflict. Ideally, it should build on structured early warning, information gathering and a careful analysis of the factors driving the conflict. Conflict prevention activities may include the use of the Secretary-General's "good offices," preventive deployment or confidence-building measures. Therefore these are the first range of options available while devising a strategy for preventive diplomacy. In the initial phase the Secretary-General may offer his "good offices" to the parties concerned for settling their dispute and perhaps even take the initiative towards devising a settlement. As a part of conflict prevention, confidence-building measures (CBMs) are designed to avert, cope and decide crises that are likely to intensify into violent conflicts between states or between states and non-state actors. To be operative, they require translucent and verifiable actions by the immediate parties to a conflict so as to establish a more predictable and a mutually satisfactory pattern of conduct. CBMs can thus be unilateral, bilateral or multilateral depending on the nature of the conflict. They are often facilitated and supported by third parties, including regional and international governmental and non-governmental organisations. CBMs can be military, diplomatic, political, or cultural in their nature and they can be applied equally in conflicts between, across, and within states. In the short term, they are designed to decelerate a crisis before major violence breaks out or to stabilise an immediate post-ceasefire situation. In the medium term, CBMs are meant to increase contact and trust between the parties to a conflict and galvanise them to a new approach in addressing their dispute. In the long term, they can play a crucial role in paving the way to, and sustaining, a meaningful conflict settlement.[3]

As regards peace keeping, it is one of the most important aspects for securing international peace and security.

Traditionally it was devised as a technique to preserve peace, no matter how fragile. And after fighting had been halted or suspended, it involved the separation of forces and to assist the implementation of the peace plan. Its importance as a tool for peace maintenance can be seen from the fact that as of November 30, 2012 there are 1,17,000 UN personnel serving in 16 separate "peacekeeping operations" (PKOs) led by the Department of Peace Keeping Operations (DPKO) in four different continents; which is a ninefold increase, since 1999. About 113 different states of the UN have contributed to the UN force, since the UN does not have any armed forces of its own. The UN budget has also increased to US$ 7.23 billion and since 1948 there have been 53 different UN peacekeeping operations.

As far as "peacekeeping" is concerned the UN has traditionally followed three basic principles. These are: (1) To take the consent of the parties to a conflict (2) Impartiality and (3) Non-use of force except when required for self-defence purposes. A UN peacekeeping operation should only use force as a measure of last resort. It should always be calibrated in a precise, proportional and appropriate manner, within the principle of the minimum force necessary to achieve the desired effect, while sustaining consent for the mission and its mandate. The use of force by a UN peacekeeping operation always has political implications and can often give rise to unforeseen circumstances. These principles, if implemented with care, have had a salutary effect on the performance of the peacekeeping forces that have averted and helped contain many a conflict. The above figures prove the utility of this method.

Another method is peace making. Under the concept of peace making it becomes important to see that conflicts that are in progress are contained and this includes taking diplomatic initiatives and even action to bring the parties involved in hostile action to a negotiated settlement. In this respect the Secretary-General can, at his own initiative, regardless of whether the Security Council or the General Assembly have authorised him or not, use his own "good offices" to bring about a settlement. Peace makers can also include not only regional organisations, but also a group of states, special envoys or even NGOs. Sometimes even influential businessmen or influential "think tanks" can be used for what is euphemistically called as "track-2" diplomacy to arrive at a settlement between the parties to a conflict.

Another method is peace enforcement. By contrast, peace enforcement does not require the consent of the main parties and may involve the use of military force at the strategic or international level, which is normally prohibited for member states under Article 2(4) of the Charter, unless authorised by the Security Council. If the Security Council does indeed give its consent and authorisation then a range of coercive measures can be considered, including the use of limited force. Included in this aspect are such options as sanctions and a reference to the International Criminal Court (ICC) of proven delinquents including state actors that do not carry out Security Council resolutions to stop obvious genocide, rape and mass murder. Such actions are authorised to restore international peace and security in situations where the Security Council has determined the existence of a threat to the peace, breach of the peace or act of aggression. The Security Council may utilise, where appropriate, regional organisations and agencies for enforcement action under its authority.

The word "sanction" does not appear anywhere in the UN Charter. However Article 39 under Chapter VII of the UN Charter states that once the UN Security Council determines that there does exist a threat or a danger to the maintenance of peace or an act of aggression, it can choose to take a range of preventive measures under Article 40, or it can take recourse to the use of force under Article 42. It is Article 41 that is important for the purposes of imposing sanctions that are non-military in nature. Sanctions are an ancient tool of economic and political coercion and have not been invented recently. Some historians have averred that the earliest sanctions case in recorded history was in 432 BC, when the city state of Athens imposed a punitive ban on Megaran traders, shortly before the start of the Peloponnesian War.[4] Sanctions have been deployed throughout history in pursuit of economic and political objectives and with increasing intensity after the First World War. The first cases of multilateral sanctions (imposed by a group of states) were deployments by the League of Nations in response to incidents of cross-border aggression by Yugoslavia (1921); Greece (1925); and Italy (1935). During the period of Cold War paralysis, the Security Council deployed sanctions only twice: trade and financial sanctions against Southern Rhodesia from 1965 to 1979 for its unilateral declaration of independence from Great Britain, and a voluntary and mandatory arms embargo in 1963 and 1977 respectively, to persuade the South African regime to end apartheid.

In the heady period of new-found unity among the five permanent members (P-5) of the UN Security Council after the end of the Cold War, beginning in 1990 until the early 2000s the Security Council deployed sanctions in two cases of cross-border aggression: on Iraq and the former Yugoslavia in 1991; and in civil war (the National Union for the Total Independence of Angola, UNITA) and civil dispute (Haiti), in 1993. The Security Council also imposed sanctions on several other state and non-state actors in Africa for actions considered as threats to, or breaches of international peace and security: Liberia and Somalia (1992); Rwanda (1994); the Revolutionary United Front (Sierra Leone, 1997); Eritrea and Ethiopia (2000, for their border dispute); and Liberia again in 2001 in response to Charles Taylor's support for the Revolutionary United Front (RUF). In the mid-2000s, the Security Council deployed sanctions on the Democratic Republic of the Congo (DRC), Côte d'Ivoire and on Sudan.[5]

Another form of sanction that is in the process of development and needs further encouragement is the criminal sanction of law. War crimes tribunals, the international criminal court (ICC), and even foreign domestic courts have deterrence potential as well as retributive power; though their processes are slow, they target only individuals, and they have difficulty getting those they indict to appear, the political impact of courts is significant and likely to increase. Indicted political and military leaders may be secure for a time in their own countries, but (as the Pinochet case showed) they will be at risk travelling abroad and can have no confidence in immunity if the leadership in their own nation changes, as eventually it is very likely to do. But here again there are obvious limitations. Can an official of a P-5 power, who has been indicted for war crimes, be ever brought to justice? The case of US officials, who behaved in an utterly uncivilised and depraved manner at the Abu Gharib jail in Iraq, will ever be tried by the ICC? It is extremely doubtful. It would seem therefore that officials of the P-5 states as also of some other leading states will never have to face justice at the hands of the ICC no matter how depraved their crimes are.

Nevertheless the question that arises is: are sanctions a successful method for deterring aggression? The first comprehensive study of the effectiveness of targeted multilateral sanctions is under way as a joint project by Thomas J. Biersteker,[6] and Sue E. Eckert.[7] However the reality may be that there is simply insufficient data available on multilateral sanctions in general and targeted sanctions in particular, to formulate any definitive conclusions about their effectiveness. Despite a seemingly unrelenting dissatisfaction and challenges, Security Council sanctions have progressed into a critical mechanism for helping to resolve intricate issues of international peace and security, including humanitarian crises. Moreover, regional partners of the UN are applying sanctions with growing dynamism, often but not always with the Council's approval. This development is basically positive as it evidences the willingness of the international community to work together to wield the necessary leverage to produce desired outcomes.

Lastly, there is the method of peace building. This involves a range of measures targeted to reduce the risk of lapsing or relapsing into conflict by strengthening national capacities at all levels for effective administrative purposes. This also means that a solid foundation has to be built for sustainable peace and development. Peace building is a complex, long-term process of creating the necessary conditions for sustainable peace. It works by addressing the deep-rooted, structural causes of violent conflict in a comprehensive manner. Peace building measures have to address the core issues that affect the functioning of society and the state, and seek to enhance the capacity of the state to effectively and legitimately carry out its core functions.[8]

Nevertheless, if all non-coercive and non-military methods have failed to restore international peace and security, then the international community has no option left but to consider the use of force as an option. However before this option is considered it is important that there should be some guidelines or principles that the international community should consider. It is not easy to consider the use of force as a simple option, for it has international ramifications. Sometimes, the results may not be in consonance with the action taken. The former Australian Foreign Minister Gareth Evans formulated the following five basic principles before considering coercive military action. These were:

- Just Cause: Is there serious and irreparable harm occurring to human beings, or imminently likely to occur, of the following kind: (a) Large-scale loss of life, actual or apprehended, with genocidal intent or not, which is the product either of deliberate state action or state neglect, inability to act, or a failed-state situation; or (b) Large-scale ethnic cleansing, actual or apprehended, whether carried out by killing, forced expulsion, acts of terror, or rape. The bar for military intervention here has been set deliberately high and tight and excludes many kinds of unconscionable behaviour for example; imprisonment and torture of political opponents or overthrow of a democratically elected government that would certainly justify other forms of coercive response for example, targeted sanctions.

- Right Intention: Is the primary purpose of the proposed military action to halt or avert human suffering, whatever other motives may be in play?
- Last Resort: Has every non-military option for the prevention or peaceful resolution of the crisis been explored, and are there reasonable grounds for believing lesser measures will not succeed? These guidelines are not intended to mean that every non-military option must literally have been tried and failed. Given that there will often be simply no time for that process to work itself out, what is necessary is that there be reasonable grounds for believing, in all the circumstances, that these other measures would not have succeeded. There are other scholars who believe that there ought to be only two criteria for initiating humanitarian military action as a last resort. These are (1) threats to international peace and security and (2) a massive violation of human rights. (Stanley Hoffmann)
- Proportional Means: Is the scale, duration, and intensity of the planned military action the minimum necessary to secure the defined human protection objective?
- Reasonable Prospects: Is there a reasonable chance of the military action being successful in meeting the threat in question, and are the consequences of action not likely to be worse than the consequences of inaction? This last balance-of-consequences test is, and should be, a very important constraint. Apart from anything else, it effectively rules out military action against any one of the five permanent members of the Security Council even if all other conditions for intervention were to be met. The same is true for other major powers. That is why Indonesia's permission was required for the East

> Timor intervention. That permission was given only very reluctantly and under much international pressure, but it was given; the case was, accordingly, not one of coercive humanitarian intervention at all. All this raises the familiar question of double-standards to which there is at present no sensible answer.[9]

The principles formulated by the former Australian Foreign Minister are fundamentally very opaque and were perhaps designed to provide an intellectual cover for intervention by the western powers. They are not principles that have been codified or accepted by the United Nations Security Council; no matter how exceptional they may be. At best they can serve only as reference points, as they also suffer from some serious maladies.

Take the question of "just cause." Firstly, who is to define what is a "just cause"? This principle basically lacks universality of response. If the issue is humanitarian then why intervene here and not there? Civil wars, persecutions, widespread torture, forced refugees and tyrannies occur almost all over the world and are not limited to one area only. Therefore, to think of a "just cause" is perhaps a flawed moral response. Would, for example, there be humanitarian intervention in Chechenya or in Tibet, since it would involve combating a P-5 power and that might mean a greater loss of life than it was intended to save? In that case "just cause" then is a limited concept and that it follows therefore that it does not apply to the permanent members of the UN Security Council. Is "just cause" then limited and only applicable to the lesser powers?

Then there is the question of who is to authorise an intervention? The UN Security Council is also an unwieldy mechanism for achieving justice, since the existence of the veto means that P-5 states are in a position to block humanitarian interventions that do not serve their interests. As Kofi Annan has acknowledged, there is no simple way to resolve this dilemma. On the other hand unilateral intervention by itself cannot have adequate legitimacy, unless it is in some significant way authorised by the United Nations. One possibility is that, when a veto is exercised, a simple majority of the Security Council or of the permanent members could confer a moral authorisation for intervention. The condition of UN authorisation should also apply to multilateral interventions, since without UN authorisation they will invariably wear the appearance of sectional bias. What is apparent here is the urgent need for Security Council membership reforms. How can the UNSC P-5 membership, which reflects the power equations that existed at the end of the Second World War, in the year 2013, take major decisions that impinge on the situation that prevails today?

The alternative devised by some western powers of "coalitions of the willing" might have certain obvious advantages, but one cannot ignore the possibility that the willingness may arise, or be understandably perceived to arise, from motives of domination or an attempt to bypass the UN system. Therefore all interventions that bypass the United Nations, at the very least, need a very strong case to rebut the presumption that they are ethically dubious[10] and designed for furthering the foreign policy goals of a particular group of powers.

Some other scholars are not convinced of the need to take military action for humanitarian purposes even *as a last resort* (emphasis added) and are critical of the need advocated by the former Australian Foreign Minister. They feel that serious effort needs to be made before even contemplating humanitarian military intervention and perhaps "coercive diplomacy" or "forceful persuasion" would always be a better option. It is their view that certain non-violent coercive measures should always be employed at most stages of a crisis, or as a crisis looms or when humanitarian disaster presents itself. This type of prevention is likely to be less costly and less damaging than the military response to the headline-grabbing disaster. It is a curious quirk of human psychology that it is easier to create support for very expensive, dramatic military efforts, especially where the risks to the interveners are low, than for cheaper non-violent activities aimed at prevention. These non-violent approaches are not guaranteed to work and they need imagination and political savvy in their implementation if they are to be successful.

There is a conflict here between different understandings of success. Should success be thought of in a short-term way as saving these lives now, or restoring the affected people to their homes, or should the criterion of success embrace longer-term objectives such as ensuring political stability and enduring safety for people in the area threatened? Clearly, both accounts of success have their attractions, but equally clearly they are in tension in that they dictate different policies and forms of intervention. In particular, the shorter-term objective is compatible with and, in some respects, suited to military procedures, whereas armed forces alone are unlikely to deliver the longer-term objectives.[11]

Also related to the question of "success" is the next question: who should determine "success" and who should determine that the time has come for the termination of the mission? One plausible answer would be that if these missions have international sanction through the medium of the UN Security Council, then it must fall within the purview of the UN Security Council to determine its final outcome. Unfortunately what happens is that the original reason for the application of force soon morphs into something else. Take the example of sanctions against Saddam's Iraq and the subsequent UN Security Council authorising force. These were designed in the initial stages to force Iraq to withdraw from Kuwait, but as soon as this was accomplished these very same resolutions were then utilised to force a regime change. It was unofficially made clear to Iraqi interlocutors that no matter what they did, no matter even if they complied *in toto* with all the requirements of the resolutions, they would not be lifted till the departure of Saddam Hussein! In other words these resolutions were being used to effect regime change and were designed to fulfil the foreign policy agendas of the western powers.

Having looked at different strategies and principles to be followed before attempting preventive diplomacy, it is obvious that there is no common understanding or a conclusion amongst scholars and international personalities on how to proceed. The fact that the international community needs some kind of "guidelines" or a code of ethics, is to state the obvious. The fact that these need to be codified so that they are internationally acceptable is also to state the obvious. It is a matter of deep concern that so far this important consensus has not been reached by the international community. The cynical view is, of course, that some important members of the international community do not wish to see a consensus evolve for that would limit their options, as also their room for manoeuvre. If the guidelines are codified then it would become imperative that they would have to be followed, for in this age of instant communication no one can escape the glare of the international print and TV media. To follow them scrupulously would also mean that the room for manipulation would be lost. It is the same cynical view that indicates why there has, so far, been no reform of the membership of the UN Security Council despite valiant attempts by some important members of the international community. This debate is likely to continue without any chance of a forward movement in the near future.

As can be discerned preventive diplomacy can only succeed if there is P-5 unanimity both within the UN Security Council and the UN system as well as a general consensus on how to proceed further. While unanimity can ensure the quick and relatively easy passage of a resolution, the important part is that it has to be implemented too. Quite often states are content to pass a resolution, but are loath to take any further action for fear of offending the state being sanctioned. Many times resolutions are never implemented. Sometimes none of the great powers wish to take sides in a dispute and therefore feel that the ends of justice have been met with the passing of a resolution. They all know that nothing will come out of this resolution.

The world is still governed by power politics. It therefore follows that powerful and important states will certainly escape any retribution no matter how serious their misadventure. Even if there has been some severe criticism outside or inside the UN system it is easily shrugged off. Thus while the concept of preventive diplomacy is laudable and its success a matter of debate, there is no doubt that the world is still very much run on the basis of old-fashioned power politics.

CASE STUDY—IRAN

The role of the UN and its principal organ for peace-keeping, the Security Council, has already been discussed as it related to the Iran-Iraq War where hardly any serious or meaningful effort was made through preventive diplomacy to halt the carnage. Even when the question of the use of chemical weapons arose, the Iranians were bitterly critical of the role played by the UN. It seemed to Iran that the UN Security Council was in thrall to the great powers and was thus unable to perform its primary task in an unbiased manner.

The Iranians are not new to the manipulations of international institutions by the great powers for their own political purposes. Following the nationalisation of the Anglo-Iranian Oil Company by the popularly elected Mossadegh government in March-April 1951, Britain imposed a world-wide embargo on Iranian oil, making it extremely difficult for Iran to sell its main export product. Britain also froze Iran's sterling assets, banned exports to Iran, reinforced British naval forces in the Gulf, entered a case against Iran in the World Court and following September lodged a complaint against Iran in the UN Security Council. PM Mossadegh came to the UN to defend Iran's case and met US President Truman to seek his help for Iran's case. Mossadegh misjudged US intentions, for although the US failed to support British efforts in the UN, yet nevertheless the US was also keen to stop nationalisation of oil companies. Failing to thwart Iranian government plans for nationalisation of its oil industry, the British government next attempted a coup that unfortunately for them failed. Eventually the US took the lead, overthrew the Mossadegh government through the auspices of a CIA coup (Operation Ajax) and insisted with the new Iranian rulers that US oil companies get an "appropriate" share of Iranian oil. Ever grateful, the new government of Iran duly obliged the US.

It was at the instigation of the US that the newly crowned Shah signed a civil nuclear agreement with the US in 1957. It is indeed a strange irony that it was the US that first encouraged the Shah of Iran's nuclear ambitions. Under the US "atoms for peace" programme the Shah was allowed in 1967 to buy a 5mw light water research reactor. Interestingly, the Bushehr nuclear facility was built not by the Russians but by Siemens! There was no word of protest then from the western powers as the Shah was deemed to be "our man" and euphemistically dubbed as the "guardian of the gulf." When Ayatollah Khomeini assumed power in Iran after the overthrow of the Shah and formed the new Iranian republic, he actually ordered the closure of Iranian nuclear facilities terming them as the "work of the devil." US-Iranian nuclear cooperation only came to an end with the overthrow of the Shah in 1979. The foundations for Iranian nuclear ambitions, if any, were laid at that time directly with US help.

The overthrow of the Shah in 1979 was a cataclysmic event for the western powers led by the US. With the departure of the Shah western policy in the Gulf region lay in tatters. What followed was even worse. US embassy personnel were taken hostage in Tehran as the US had allowed the Shah to enter the US on "medical" grounds.

The UNSC passed resolution 457 on December 4, 1979 and a further resolution 461 on December 31, 1979 calling for the immediate release of American hostages. Iran ignored these UNSC resolutions. When the US then sought to impose sanctions on Iran by passing a UNSC resolution, this was vetoed by the then Soviet Union. UN Secretary-General, Waldheim then visited Iran in order to seek the release of American hostages, but this visit yielded no result. The UN Secretary-General offered his "good offices" and even agreed to a UN Commission of inquiry on Iran's alleged grievances against the Shah. Although the UN Commission included countries such as Algeria and Syria, it yielded little result to the satisfaction of Iran.

The US response to the Shah's overthrow and the subsequent hostage crisis has been described in detail in the chapter on Iraq. US-Iran relations have never recovered from this point onwards. Nevertheless, the US imposed broad economic sanctions against Iran and clearly the roots lie in the hostage crisis of 1979. On November 14, 1979 President Carter ordered a "freeze" on all Iranian assets which were subject to the jurisdiction of the US government. Additional sanctions were imposed when the US suspected Iran of complicity in the bombing of the US Marine base in Lebanon. The US also accused Iran of supporting the Lebanon based Hezbollah. Steadily these sanctions have been tightened with the US accusing Iran of not only supporting terrorism, but also of having ambitions for developing nuclear weapons. The main US concern is the fear that Iran was developing nuclear weapons capability. This would, in the US view, present it with an unacceptable strategic risk.

Not to be left behind the EU has also imposed sanctions on Iran, although these are of recent origin. In January 2012 the EU announced an oil embargo on Iran beginning July 1, 2012. According to the EU Trade Commission Iran exported in 2011 goods worth US$ 19 billion to the EU countries and 90 per cent of these were petroleum products. Earlier in June 2010 the EU, in line with measures adopted by the US Congress, banned assistance and investment to Iran's energy sector. A series of prohibitions were also placed on European firms doing business with Iran. The EU also targeted banks, designated individuals, companies and other organisations for sanctions. All these measures were designed to force Iran to come to the bargaining table to halt its efforts towards nuclear weapons capability. The EU and the US were acting in tandem in this regard.

There are altogether 6 United Nations Security Council Resolutions that seek to address the issue of Iran's nuclear ambitions. The central demand of the UN Security Council is that Iran suspend its nuclear enrichment programme and undertake "confidence building measures" as underlined by the IAEA Board of Governors Resolution of February 2006. These confidence building measures include Iran reconsidering construction of heavy water reactor and that it ratify IAEA additional protocol. In March 2006 a non-binding Presidential statement was issued outlining the above course of action and urging Iran to adopt it. The 6 UNSC Resolutions are:

On July 31, 2006 the UN Security Council passed resolution 1696 under Article 40 of the UN Charter while endorsing the P-5 and German offer of diplomatic and economic incentives; warned Iran to comply with IAEA Board of Governors report of February 2006 by

August 31, 2006. Iran failed to comply with UN Security Council's earlier demands as set forth in resolution 1696 and therefore on December 23, 2006 the UNSC further unanimously passed another resolution 1737 under Article 41 of the UN Charter. This resolution urged Iran to comply with Resolution 1696. On March 24, 2007 UNSC passed another resolution 1747 under Article 41 of the UN Charter that "encouraged" Iran to reach a long term comprehensive agreement with the P-5 + Germany. As no further progress seemed to take place yet another UN resolution 1803 was passed on March 3, 2008 that essentially reiterated the earlier sanctions. For the first time a UNSC resolution 1835 that was not passed under Chapter VII underlined the UNSC's commitment to "an early negotiated solution to the Iran nuclear issue" and therefore recommended no new sanctions. As no further progress was made, the UNSC passed resolution 1929 on June 9, 2010 under UN Charter Article 41 that imposed a complete arms embargo and instituted an inspection regime to enforce the resolution.

By the end of 2010 it became quite clear that the UNSC had reached an impasse. Both Russia and China were reluctant to institute any further UNSC mandated sanctions against Iran. Both are veto holding powers. On January 18, 2012 the Russian Foreign Minister Lavrov publicly informed that the scope of sanctions over Iran's nuclear programme had been exhausted and that any additional measures were now designed to "provoke discontent" in Iran. Without publicly saying so the message was clear. Russia was not interested in a "regime change" that the western powers were working towards. When the US instituted its own sanctions that included an oil embargo,

China publicly stated that a "country's domestic law could not be above international law and that the US could not force other countries to adopt it." Similarly Turkey also refused to adopt the unilaterally sponsored US embargo.

When the 27 nation European Union, in conjunction with the measures already taken by the US, decided to place an oil embargo on Iran effective from July 1, 2012, little did they envisage that the success or failure of their gambit would largely depend upon China's attitude. It is entirely possible that the EU, suffering from a severe economic compression, took this huge gamble in the hope that this action would induce Iran to come to the negotiating table to discuss its nuclear weapons ambitions. The more optimistic and perhaps facile hope was that Iran might actually move away from the actual production of nuclear weapons. Whether the refusal to buy Iranian oil, as envisaged by the EU embargo, actually induces Iran to change policy or affects a regime change, as sanguinely hoped by the west, remains to be seen. The Iranians have probably not forgotten that the democratically elected government of PM Mossadegh was overthrown by the US and UK on the basis of a CIA sponsored coup (Operation Ajax) that eventually led to the installation of the Shah.

In the past China has assisted Iran in the development of its nuclear programme, but it must be admitted that most of this assistance was in the civilian sector. However sometimes there can be dual use of such technology as with the help given in enrichment of uranium process. Between 1985 and 1996 China provided Iran with critical nuclear technology that helped Iran master the uses of lasers for uranium enrichment. Chinese technicians and engineers trained Iranian nuclear scientists at the Esfahan Nuclear

Research Centre which was to later play an important part in the development of Iranian nuclear programme.[1] Officially however the Chinese maintain that Iran should "show flexibility and sincerity and have earnest cooperation with the IAEA."[2]

The EU imports approximately 25 per cent of total Iranian oil exports. Within the EU the three major importers are Italy, Spain and Greece, all with very fragile economies. It is interesting that the date from which the EU decision became effective, July 1, 2012, was calculated in the hope that the situation in Libya would stabilise by then so that the loss of Iranian supplies could be adequately compensated by supplies from Libya. If the EU continues to refuse to purchase Iranian oil any further, then the alternative for Iran is to divert such a surplus to major oil importing Asian countries.

There are four major oil consuming countries in Asia. The largest consumer of Iranian oil is China which imports about 22 per cent of Iranian crude, followed by Japan with 14 per cent, India about 12 per cent and South Korea about 10 per cent. Of the four countries, both Japan and South Korea might be inclined to follow the western line due to their very close security and economic links with the US, and the continuing problems that they face with China and North Korea respectively. India has found the situation extremely delicate and is in the process of finding a via media in the hope of not upsetting either of the two parties. India has been strongly urging for a diplomatic solution fearing that any flare-up would send the price of crude skyrocketing northwards with consequent sharp ill-effects on its economy. There are reports however that India might conclude a swap arrangement by which the payment for Iranian crude may be made in rupees and partially in gold. Two Banks are mentioned in this context, the UCO Bank of India and the Turkish Bank, Halk Bankasi.[3]

As China's demand and consumption of oil is huge, China is but naturally interested in Iranian energy resources. Both China and Iran have formed a joint oil and gas committee to broaden and expedite energy cooperation. China is also an important investor in "upstream" Iranian oil operations (exploration/extraction). China is slated to develop the giant Azadegan and Yadavaran oil and natural gas fields. Although in 2011 total volume of Iranian-China trade amounted to US$ 39 billion, yet new Chinese investments amounted to US$ 1 billion. Since 2007 China is Iran's largest trading partner.

There are reports that officials of the Chinese oil giant SINOPEC are already negotiating with officials of the Iranian National Oil Company (INOC) for further major discounts on future oil imports. Ostensibly the purpose is to purchase Iranian oil on the cheap so as to build up healthy Chinese strategic oil reserves. Two Chinese companies, SINOPEC and China National Petroleum Co., have large exploration contracts with Iran on developing the Yadavaran and South Pars oilfields. Thus the Chinese stake in Iran is considerable.[4]

Nevertheless the Chinese will have to balance their energy relationship with Iran with their interests in maintaining a solid working relationship with the US. In the past two years, two Chinese firms CNOOC and SINOPEC have invested US$4.6 billion in energy assets in the US.[5] The EU decision to place an oil embargo on Iran by itself has little meaning for the Chinese, for EU countries singly or collectively, are in no position to influence the Chinese.

It is the relationship with the US that worries the Chinese. The US has in recent times passed the "Comprehensive Iran Sanctions, Accountability and Divestment Act 2010" which empowers the US Administration to prevent any company that trades with Iran from receiving US Export Licences or to borrow more than US$ 10 million from a US Bank. A Chinese company, Zuhai Zhenrong was penalised for trading in oil with Iran. Similarly the US passed the "National Defence Authorisation Act 2012" that authorises the Administration to penalise any company that deals with the Iranian Central Bank. It is through the Central Bank that all deals are settled. If the US can persuade the Chinese to toe the western line, the days for Iran are numbered.

If on the other hand China decides to keep its relationship intact with the Iranians despite US pressure, it is in a position to do so. All it has to do is to purchase Iranian oil and offset this against a supply of essential consumer goods from China to Iran and to settle the accounts in Chinese Yuan. This is already happening. On March 21, 2013 a Chinese supertanker "Yuan Yang Hu" belonging to the China Ocean Shipping Group berthed at Kharg island (Iranian oil port) to load about 2m/b of crude destined for China. This was for the first time since the imposition of the EU embargo that a Chinese supertanker had arrived to lift oil from Iran. A spokesperson of the Chinese Foreign Ministry Hong Lei clarified that "China maintains normal and transparent energy cooperation with Iran in accordance with its own energy requirements." China further clarified that "we obviously oppose some country imposing sanctions against another country according to their own domestic law."

Thus as can be seen in the case of Iran, preventive diplomacy has been largely absent. So far neither the UN

Security Council nor the US have stipulated the precise criteria that Iran must meet in order for the sanctions to be lifted. There is no action plan that is clearly understood by all the parties. And therefore even if Iran were to move forward in the desired direction, what is the plan for unwinding the plethora of legislation instituting the sanctions? To some observers it would seem a repetition of the Iraq sanctions. Whenever Saddam complied with some "demands" of the western powers acting under the aegis of the "international community," the goal post was then unilaterally shifted. Eventually in the case of Saddam's Iraq nothing short of a regime change would prove to be sufficient. Is Iran headed in the same direction?

The Iranians have been critical of the role of the UN Secretary-General Ban Ki-moon. On February 15, 2013 Ban Ki-moon told the *Washington Post* that "the UN must be swift in judging whether diplomacy can resolve world concerns about Iran's nuclear programme, or invite the risk that Iran will use talks as a cover to build a bomb." Not unnaturally the Iranian Ambassador to the UN, Khazaei protested and called upon the UN Secretary-General to maintain "impartiality."[6] To be fair however Ban Ki-moon went to Tehran to attend the Non-Aligned Conference despite US and Israeli pressure not to do so. He met most of the Iranian leadership but did take positions that were decidedly pro West. Efforts undertaken on behalf of the UN Secretary-General, or by him personally, have been half-hearted and whenever the interests of the great powers has come into play, the effort has been stymied. The present UN Secretary-General's role has indeed been contentious.

Although there are UN Security Council Resolutions on the table, yet to implement them requires unanimity amongst the P-5 powers which has been lacking. Sanctions are at best a tool of coercive diplomacy and can only be considered to be effective if they ultimately achieve a real change of policy. With Russia and China refusing to add an oil embargo to the list of UN sanctions, there is little that the western powers can do except institute sanctions of their own. And this is precisely what the western powers have done. These sanctions are not sanctioned by the internal community and are unilateral in nature. Therefore the issue at stake is, what will other great powers like China do? Chinese support is crucial for Iran to continue to defy western pressure in the form of sanctions. On balance unilateral sanctions against Iran have so far only contributed to a worsening of relations between Iran and the western powers. To the general Iranian public these sanctions are seen as "economic warfare" by the west. Rather than destabilising the regime it will only entrench them further. The west should have learned the lesson of the sanctions regime instituted against Iraq that only ended up in strengthening the Saddam regime. Iran, which is by far the most important country in the Middle East, has neither stopped its nuclear weapons development programme nor has it lessened its support for Hezbollah in Lebanon. In the oil industry circles in the US there continues to be the feeling that active engagement with Iran would yield better results than confrontation.[7] Gen. James Mattis of the US Central Command told the US Senate Armed Forces Committee that the "current" diplomatic and economic sanctions against Iran were "not working."[8]

There is a belief amongst some Chinese analysts in Beijing that continuing "confrontation" between Iran and the US is to the strategic benefit to China. They feel that the US, distracted and bogged down in the Middle East, would be incapable of focusing attention to the growing power of China in Asia. This in turn would pave the way for China to emerge as a superpower in the near future. Such analysts draw inspiration from a prominent Chinese foreign policy analyst, Wang Jisi, Dean of the Beijing University School of International Studies who has argued that "China benefited from the US war in Iraq as it is beneficial for our external environment to have the US militarily and diplomatically deeply sunk in the Middle East to the extent that it can hardly extricate itself." Similarly Renmin University Professor Shi Yinhong has argued that "Washington's deeper involvement in the Middle East is favourable to Beijing reducing Washington's ability to place focused attention and pressure on China."[9] This also means that US attempts to "re-balance" back to the Asia-Pacific region would probably have to be postponed.

Thus the crucial factor is what China does. In the UN Security Council a stalemate exists with both Russia and China reluctant to take any further punitive measure against Iran.

The election of the moderate Rowhani to the Iranian Presidency was an important factor and an opening leading to a thaw is possible that may not lead to confrontation between the Western powers and Iran. The on going contacts established at the UN were quickly followed by secret bilateral diplomacy between Iran and the United States which resulted in a partial agreement at Geneva. Much work still needs to be done for as per the present understanding only a six month breathing space is available; with hard liners on both sides adamant that there should be no compromise.

Below is a list of UN Security Council resolutions issued against Iran. The Security Council established a Committee pursuant to Resolution 1737 that monitors resolutions relating to Iran.

Resolution	Date Passed	Measures
1929	June 9, 2010	Expresses concern about Iran's lack of compliance with previous resolutions, expands and reinforces sanctions, including restrictions on arms, finance, shipping and other "proliferation sensitive activities." Calls upon all states to take measures to prevent the transfer to Iran of weapons systems, and to report on the measures they have taken to implement the sanctions. This resolution was met with strong opposition from Turkey and Brazil, who tried to engineer a nuclear fuel swap deal.
1835	September 27, 2008	Reaffirms previous resolutions that approved sanctions and demanded that Iran stop uranium enrichment in light of a September 15 IAEA report that Iran had failed to comply with these demands. Indonesia declared its opposition to further sanctions by stating that had Resolution 1835 included further sanctions, it would not have voted in favour.

1803	March 3, 2008	Extends sanctions against Iran. Notes that the Iranian government attempts to enrich uranium—potentially a key component in the development of nuclear weapons. Restricts the import of "dual use" technology used for both peaceful and military purposes, and asks UN member states to inspect cargos suspected of transporting nuclear material to and from Iran. Adds 13 names to an existing travel ban and asset freeze on companies and individuals thought to be engaged in Iran's nuclear programme.
1747	March 24, 2007	Builds on Council's previous decision to impose sanctions on Tehran by banning Iranian arms exports and imposing a freeze on the financial assets of 28 individuals and entities. Includes mechanisms for future negotiation with Iran and reference to a nuclear-free Middle East. Concerns were expressed by South Africa, Indonesia and Qatar over the right of parties to the NPT to peaceful uses of nuclear technology.
1737	December 23, 2006	Imposes sanctions against Iran. Calls for compliance with IAEA requirements, bans trade with Iran of all items, materials, equipment, goods and technology which could contribute to Tehran's uranium enrichment programme and contains a list of persons and entities targeted with an assets freeze. Establishes a new sanctions committee to monitor compliance of the resolution.

1696	June 31, 2006	Endorses the offer of diplomatic and economic incentives put forward by the P5 and Germany and demands that Iran suspend all uranium enrichment programmes by August 31. Acts under Article 40 of Chapter VII of the United Nations in order to make mandatory the suspension required by the IAEA. Threatens Iran with sanctions in case of non-compliance but avoids any implication that use of force may be warranted. Iran rejected the resolution claiming that it has only made negotiations more difficult.

Source: Global Policy Forum

CASE STUDY—IRAQ

In the last two or three decades Iraq was involved in three conflicts. These were the Iran-Iraq War, the First Gulf War involving the invasion of Kuwait and expulsion of Iraqi troops from Kuwait and the Second Gulf War involving the invasion of Iraq by a group of western countries led by the United States. In each case let us examine whether preventive diplomacy could have prevented conflict, and as the conflict progressed whether it could have contained the fighting, and whether it could have enforced a ceasefire amongst the belligerents. And if preventive diplomacy failed in this case what were the reasons for its failure?

The Iran-Iraq War (1980-88)

On September 22, 1980 Iraq launched an all-out attack on Iran having earlier on September 17, 1980 abrogated the 1975 Algiers Treaty that had settled the Iraqi-Iranian boundary. The very act of Iraqi aggression against Iran was not unknown to the outside world for previous to this date tension had been steadily building between the two countries. Border skirmishes had broken out earlier by autumn of 1980. On September 7, 1980 Iraqi forces forcibly occupied the area of Zain al-Qaws. Saddam Hussein of Iraq was under the impression that the Iranian revolution had sufficiently weakened the Iranian army and that it was facing a shortage of critical US spare parts. Most of its top generals had been cashiered under the Ayatollah regime and some who had fled to Iraq gave exaggerated accounts of the collapse of morale amongst its officer corps. Saddam was also fed doctored intelligence by the US through the Saudis to the same tune. As the *Financial Times* noted, "US intelligence and satellite data showed that the Iranians would break." Saddam was also encouraged by the US to launch his aggression and President Carter gave Saddam the "green light."[1]

Not only was no preventive diplomatic action undertaken, but the UN Security Council waited for four full days after the commencement of hostilities before even holding a meeting! Thus between September 26, 1980 and October 24, 1980 the UN Security Council met six times. It was only on the second meeting on September 28, 1980 that it passed UN Security Council Resolution 479 that called for an end to the fighting. Significantly, Resolution 479 did not condemn or even mention Iraqi aggression and nor did it call for forces to return to internationally recognised borders. Iran rightly rejected this resolution as being completely one-sided, as it so was. As a protest against the perceived partisan attitude of the UN Security Council, Iran thereafter was to boycott its proceedings till July 5, 1988. To make amends somewhat the UN Secretary-General Kurt Waldheim at first offered his "good offices" and when that did not find any takers, he appointed Olaf Palme as his special representative in November 1980, but his mission too was a failure. The failure was entirely due to the fact that the Iranians did not trust Kurt Waldheim for his alleged "closeness" to the Shah of Iran and the fact that his dealings in the hostage crisis were seen by the Iranians as being partisan. Meanwhile the fighting continued.

The UN Security Council was not to meet again formally till July 12, 1982. Given its biased approach, the

UN Security Council now called for a "return" to pre-war boundaries for by then the Iraqis were losing the war as the Iranians had expelled all the Iraqi forces from Iranian territory and were near to overrunning southern Iraq. Only 10 resolutions were adopted by the Security Council during 8 years of Iran-Iraq War. All of them, except for Resolution 598, described the war as a *situation* between Iran and Iraq and not as the Iran-Iraq *war*, which would have been very important from the viewpoint of international law and the Charter of the United Nations. Meanwhile, Iran had resorted to its inalienable right of legitimate defence in line with Article 51 of the Charter of the United Nations as Iraq was the country that had started, continued and expanded the scope of war. According to Article 39 of the Charter of the United Nations, in case of an act of aggression, the Security Council should first make sure about the aggression and then take steps according to Articles 41 and 42 of the Charter. Naturally, not recognising Iraq as aggressor by the Security Council and not condemning that country was per se a violation of Article 39 of the Charter.

Resolution 598 remained silent on how the war began and how the invasion occurred, thus trying to imply that if Iraq was responsible for the beginning of war, Iran was definitely responsible for its continuation. Iran was denied satisfaction when Resolution 598 refused to name Iraq as the aggressor. Nevertheless as Iraq appeared in danger of a collapse despite massive Arab and US support, the UN Security Council in 1987 passed Resolution 598 under Articles 39 and 40 of Chapter VII giving itself the authority to use "force" in case either of the belligerents refused to implement the decision. While very reluctantly accepting the Resolution, Iran dubbed it as "a vicious American manoeuvre."[2]

Strangely, *it was not till December 9, 1991 that the UN Secretary-General summoned sufficient courage to name Iraq as the "aggressor"* in the Iran-Iraq War, but that was because by then the international environment had changed completely to Iraq's disadvantage and Iraq was now considered as an "enemy" by the US for its invasion and subsequent expulsion from Kuwait by US-led forces!

The decision taken by Saddam to attack Iran *was not seen by the US as confirmation of any aggressive intent on the part of the Iraqi authorities, but more as an effort to oppose the Iranian revolution and to secure the position of the oil rich pro-US Gulf monarchies* (emphasis added). The failure of "Operation Eagle Claw" to rescue US hostages from Tehran also rankled heavily on President Carter's mind, who facing re-election, saw Saddam's aggression as an opportunity to "teach" the Ayatollahs a lesson. Wary of militarily intervening directly themselves, as the painful lessons of the Vietnam War were still fresh in the minds of the Americans, they opted for the easier option of encouraging Saddam to attack Iran.

Iranian official history records that Iraq first used chemical weapons against its soldiers on January 13, 1981. Between December 28, 1980 and March 20, 1984 Iranians list 63 separate gas attacks by the Iraqis.[3] There is no doubt that the US was acutely aware of what was going on. In a Memorandum on November 1, 1983, officials of the State Department warned the then Secretary of State Schultz that they had information that the Iraqis were using chemical weapons on an "almost daily" basis. Equally blunt was the warning that Iraq had acquired chemical weapons capability from Western firms, including possibly from a US subsidiary. The US was also aware that chemical weapons were being used against "Kurdish insurgents." At the same time the US continued to provide Iraq with critical battle planning assistance and satellite data on Iranian military movements, knowing very well that Iraq was using chemical weapons against Iran as also Kurdish insurgents.[4] By 1986, the CIA also established a direct "Washington to Baghdad" link to provide the Iraqis "faster" intelligence from US satellites. Reportedly more than sixty DIA officers were now deployed to help the Iraqis![5]

However, the US gave a clear indication that it was not going to do anything, when it was announced shortly thereafter that Donald Rumsfeld would be visiting Baghdad as a "special" representative of the President. The significance and the timing of the Rumsfeld visit were to publicly announce to the world that the US supported Saddam. On December 20, 1983, Rumsfeld had a 90-minute meeting with Saddam Hussein. Rumsfeld handed over a letter to Saddam from President Reagan. In this meeting, subjects discussed were common Iraq-US interests and an opposition to an outcome of the Iran-Iraq War that *weakened Iraq's role or enhanced the ambitions of Iran* (emphasis added). De-classified documents show that Rumsfeld made no reference to chemical weapons or their use by Iraq. He was much later to deny this, but by then the whole situation had changed.

As could be expected the Iraqis were extremely pleased with the visit and the US tilt towards Iraq continued unabated. Rumsfeld made a second visit to Iraq on March 24, 1984. Coincidentally, on the same day the UN released a report that Iraq had used mustard gas and tabun nerve agents against Iranian troops. Undeterred by this news, the *New York Times* of March 29, 1984 quoted a US diplomat in Baghdad to say that they were completely "satisfied" with Rumsfeld's second visit! On the military side, the US directly allowed the sale of "civilian" helicopters to Iraq. The US secretly urged, in violation of US law, Saudi Arabia, Jordan, Kuwait and Egypt to "transfer" US origin military equipment with them to Iraq.[6] To help Iraq the US had no hesitation in identifying the foreign sources of Iranian military supplies and trying to staunch this flow. This effort was dubbed as "Operation Staunch." This was a little disingenuous and a sign of bad faith for the US itself, through Israel, had been clandestinely supplying arms and vital spares to Iran (cf. the Iran-Contra affair). The US was not averse to playing both sides.

Nevertheless, the US could not keep the lid on the use by Iraq of chemical weapons without seriously jeopardising its own standing in the world. Aware that Iraq was using chemical weapons the State Department briefing on February 24, 1984 quoted an Iraqi military statement as follows: "The invaders (Iranian) should know that for every harmful insect there is an insecticide capable of annihilation ... and Iraq possesses this insecticide." Further on March 6, 1984 the State Department announced that, based on available evidence, it "concluded" that Iraq had used lethal chemical weapons in the fighting with Iran. To soften the blow to the Iraqis the US also criticised the Iranians as follows:

> While condemning Iraq's resort to chemical weapons, the United States also calls on the government of Iran to accept the good offices proffered by a number of countries and

> international organisations to put an end to the bloodshed. The United States finds the present Iranian regime's intransigent refusal to deviate from its avowed objective of eliminating the legitimate government of neighbouring Iraq to be inconsistent with the accepted norms of behaviour among nations and the moral and religious basis which it claims.

However the Iranians were one step ahead, for by then Iran had even produced photographs, in every gory detail, of the casualties caused by chemical weapons. By March 1984, Iran had sent about 50 soldiers suffering from chemical weapons attacks to hospitals in some European countries in order to graphically display the results of Iraqi chemical weapons use and to arouse public opinion around the world. At Iran's request the UN sent an investigation team to the region beginning March 1984. In its report of March 26, 1984, the UN team confirmed the use of chemical weapons by Iraq.

To contain the damage, the US now changed tactics and began to blame *both* Iraq and Iran. This was as a result of National Security Directive No. 139 of April 5, 1984 issued by President Reagan. It reads as follows:

> "The Secretary of State will ensure that the policy of the United States government condemning the use of chemical warfare (CW) munitions in the Iran-Iraq War is unambiguous and consistent with the 1925 Geneva Protocol. Our condemnation of the use of CW munitions by the belligerents should place equal stress on the urgent need to dissuade Iran from continuing the ruthless and inhumane tactics which have characterised recent offensives." What is

of significance is the last sentence which seeks to place equal blame on the hapless Iranians!

Further a US State Department press release emphasised that "the US finds the Iranian regime's intransigent refusal to deviate from its avowed objective of eliminating the legitimate government of Iraq to be inconsistent with expected norms!" Following President Reagan's clear directive to prevent an Iranian military victory and in spite of the clear evidence of use of chemical weapons by the Iraqis, the CIA a few months later in July 1984, began to give the Iraqis the necessary intelligence to calibrate its mustard gas attacks on Iranian troops.[7] Fully aware of all this incriminating evidence, the US still had no hesitation in establishing full diplomatic relations with Iraq on November 26, 1984. The US was in no mood to give up its objectives, or see Iraq defeated.

In the UN Security Council, the US played the by now familiar role of downplaying Iraqi complicity. While Iran continued to publicise Iraq's flagrant and blatant use of chemical weapons, the Western powers continued to show disinterest and were not even willing to recognise the gravity of the situation. Between 1984 and 1991, the UN Security Council passed sixteen resolutions in all, directly or indirectly concerning the Iran-Iraq War. In 1984, UNSC Resolution 552 did not refer to the "use of chemical weapons," despite the fact that the findings of the UN Commission were available. During the whole of 1985 the UNSC did not pass any resolution on the Iran-Iraq War, much less refer to the use of chemical weapons.

On the issue of the use of chemical weapons the UN Security Council, at first, dithered and passed no resolution. Finally a good two years later, the UNSC summoned sufficient courage and passed on March 21, 1986 a Declaration (Note: Not a Resolution). The Declaration, issued after overwhelming evidence could no longer be ignored at the cost of its credibility, stated that "chemical weapons had been used by Iraqi forces against Iranian troops and that members of the UNSC strongly condemned the confirmed use of chemical weapons in clear violation of the Geneva Protocols of 1925." Interestingly, *the US abstained from this Declaration!* (emphasis added.) To be fair to the US, they had been sending messages to the Iraqi government, however mild, that it (the Iraqis) should desist from using chemical weapons.

In March 1986, the UN Expert Commission had concluded that Iraq had used chemical weapons, yet UNSC Resolution 582 (February 24, 1986) symmetrically noted that both Iran and Iraq are signatories to the Geneva Protocol of 1925 and "deplored" in general the use of chemical weapons as being contrary to the Geneva Protocol of 1925. UNSC Resolution 588 of 1986 also did not mention use of chemical weapons, but only asked that Resolution 582 be implemented. In July 1987, UNSC Resolution 598 again deplored the use of chemical weapons as "contrary" to the Geneva Protocol of 1925, but did not elaborate, let alone name, Iraq as the guilty party. After considering the report of the Experts Committee of April 25, 1988, all that the UNSC did was to state its "dismay" in Resolution 612. Not unsurprisingly, UNSC Resolution 612 only "vigorously condemned use of chemical weapons by *both* sides." Iraq was never singled out for condemnation.

However, the UNSC did also affirm the necessity that all parties observe the Geneva Protocol of 1925. The

UNSC Resolution 619 of 1988, which primarily focused on implementing the UN Iran-Iraq Military Observer Group, did not mention chemical weapons. After the Iran-Iraq ceasefire came into effect, the UNSC considered the reports of the Experts Committee and stated in UNSC Resolution 620, that it was deeply dismayed by the continued use of chemical weapons and that it was aware that such use against the Iranians had become "more frequent." However, it may be noted that despite the new language used, it did not condemn the Iraqis. All the four subsequent UNSC resolutions passed on the Iran-Iraq situation pertained to the military situation. There was no reference to the use of chemical weapons.

The Iranian Foreign Minister Velayati could only bitterly complain, "this irresponsible and indifferent attitude of the Security Council has indeed encouraged and emboldened Iraq. ... What is the effect of these crimes on the one hand and the silence of the UN on the other?" As the US made sure that there was no condemnation of Iraq by name, it was left to the UNSC to issue non-binding "Presidential Statements" to condemn Iraq. In any case, these non-binding statements are not subject to veto by the permanent members. For example, the US made sure that the Dutch sponsored Presidential Statement of March 30, 1984 contained all the three elements that the Iraqis wanted.

On March 21, 1986, another non-binding "Presidential Statement" was issued that condemned Iraq by name for the use of chemical weapons. *Interestingly, the US was the only country that voted against this statement. The UK abstained.* (Emphasis added). A similar statement was issued on May 14, 1987. Iraq had much to be grateful for and this had a positive impact on the growing friendship between the two countries.

An estimated one million men died in the war. It had a devastating effect on both countries. The CIA estimated that Iraq suffered 382,000 military casualties—127,000 dead and 255,000 wounded or about 2.3 per cent of the total population! Another 60,000 Iraqis were made POWs. No significant territory changed hands as a result of the war. The Iraqi economy lay completely shattered. The Iranian economy, although much larger than the Iraqi, too suffered enormously. Both sides had spent nearly US$ 1.5bn per month on the war. Iraq had run up enormous foreign debts. All its foreign assets were wiped out. In 1980, Iraq had US$ 36 billion in assets, but by the end of the war its debts to non-Arab governments and banks stood at a staggering US$ 45 billion. Oil terminals at Abadan (Iran) and Basra (Iraq) were destroyed. Iraq's oil production fell from about 3 million b/d* just prior to the commencement of the war, to 550,000 b/d after the war. Iran's oil production similarly suffered. It fell from 4 million b/d before the commencement of the war, to less than 600,000 b/d on the conclusion of the war.[8] Both countries had fought themselves to total exhaustion and utter devastation.

There is no doubt that the Iran-Iraq War provided the UN Security Council with an opportunity to test its capacity for undertaking its primary task—the prevention of conflict and the maintenance of peace and security. That it was found wanting has also been clearly established. Similarly, other international organisations such as the Non-Aligned Movement [NAM] or the Organisation of Islamic Countries [OIC] too failed in their primary duty of preventing conflicts

* b/d: Barrels per day.
1 ton by crude oil is equal to 7-76 barrels.

from spreading amongst fellow members. These organisations also failed to contain the conflict or to evolve a peace formula that was acceptable to both the belligerents. The evidence is clear that great power interests usually prevail. Take for example the Argentinian invasion of the Falklands islands in 1982. The Argentine invasion was not only condemned by a Security Council Resolution, but Argentina was asked to withdraw its troops from the Falklands, unlike the case of Iraq when it attacked Iran in 1980.

While it is true that Iran may have offended international opinion, custom and morality during the hostage crisis, yet it cannot be anybody's case that it deserved *less protection* (emphasis added) from international organisations, specifically so tasked, in case of aggression against it. Playing partisan politics would only harm the credibility of the international organisation, such as the UN Security Council, in the long run. For effective action it is imperative that two conditions must be met. The first is that the parties to the dispute should be willing to refer their case to the UN and the second is that there should be some basic "understanding" amongst the great powers on how to deal with the issue. A case in point is that the war in Vietnam was never on the agenda of the Security Council and all the negotiations to end the conflict took place outside the UN system.

Iran never felt comfortable with the role played by the UN in this war. It felt that the UN was too much in thrall to the United States and that it would never get "justice" from this international organisation. As this study shows, the ultimate failure of the UN Security Council to act was largely a result of the fact that one of the superpowers was not interested in any meaningful action, since it had been a party to the encouragement of Iraq to launch hostilities against Iran. The other superpower, the then Soviet Union, involved with its own intervention in Afghanistan, was also hardly likely to take any initiative to contain the conflict. In any case it was miffed at the Iranians for having criticised its intervention in Afghanistan. Within days of its intervention the Iranian Foreign Ministry issued statement in Tehran that, "Afghanistan is a Muslim country and ... the military intervention of the government of the Soviet Union in the neighbouring country of our co-religionists is considered a hostile measure ... against all the Muslims of the world." And a little later the Iranian Foreign Minister, Sadegh Ghotbzadeh, was publicly informing the world press that Iran would give arms to the rebels if the Soviet Union did not withdraw![9] Thus neither of the two superpowers was inclined to see that hostilities against Iran end and therefore it was extremely difficult for the UN Security Council to take any action.

The First Gulf War (1990-91) Let us now examine what happened just prior to the First Gulf War and whether any effective preventive action could have been taken to prevent this conflict. By the end of the Iran-Iraq War, the US had become a major trading partner of Iraq. Annual trade between the two countries grew from about US$ 500 million in early 1980 to almost US$ 3.5 billion by 1990. Iraq was also a major market for US agricultural goods. The agricultural lobby in the US created sufficient domestic pressures in the US to induce it to continue its policy tilt towards Iraq. The end of the war with Iran was an opportune time for the US to "re-assess" its policies towards Iraq. If the US was concerned with the brutalities of Saddam or his policies, the time to act was now. Both Iran and Iraq were totally exhausted by the war and were not in any position to challenge US strategic interests. And yet publicly the US chose not to do anything. On the surface the same pro-Iraqi tilt was evident. Even in the most blatant case of "gassing" the Kurds at Halabja, the prevarication of the US was evident. Well aware of what had happened at Halabja, the US decision to send a message of support on October 12, 1989, some thirteen months later, through DPM Tariq Aziz to Saddam Hussein, can only be described as an extreme exercise of brazen self-interest. The message sent by Secretary of State Baker on behalf of President Bush was one of forthright support. The message read as follows:

> The US seeks a broadened and deepened relationship with Iraq on the basis of mutual respect. That is the policy of the President. In this regard, the President has asked me to say to you and through you to President Hussein, in the most direct way possible, that the US is not involved in any effort to weaken or destabilise Iraq. I can tell you this with the highest authority.[10]

A similar message was passed by Prince Bandar of Saudi Arabia from President Bush to Saddam Hussein in April 1990.[11] And yet the US policymakers were having second thoughts on the support of Saddam Hussein.

As far back as 1989, CENTCOM assessed that Iraq would be the next likely regional threat in the wake of the Iran-Iraq War and the decline of the Soviet threat.[12] It is inconceivable that the military and political leadership in Washington was unaware of this assessment. As early as February 1990, "war games" held by Naval War College (NWC) Strategic Studies Group envisaged an Iraqi invasion of the Arabian Peninsula. A January 12, 1990 document prepared by the State Department Planning Section entitled "Thinking about a Policy for Iraq" reflected this momentous shift in US foreign policy. The document noted:

> In the past, the US approach towards Iraq was set—almost exclusively—within an East-West context ... for the US, the starting point is oil.

The document noted important reasons why the US could not ultimately rely on the Saddam regime as it had on the Shah during the 1970s. It said, "the US was comfortable with actively supporting the Iranian build up in the 1970s because (1) we trusted Iran and (2) Iran was willing and able to assume the role of defender of our oil interests." The US trust in Iran was based on mutually shared perceptions on the nature of the Soviet threat, about the need to preserve the political status quo in the Gulf, and about the importance of Israel's security. Iraq could not play this role. The document concluded by calling for a "confrontational" approach to US-Iraq relations, noting that a "key objective" would be to "force Saddam to make hard choices."

Saddam also provoked the pro-Israeli lobby in the US by foolishly positioning missile launchers in the Western Desert so as to threaten Israel. On April 2, 1990, Saddam made a further blunder by publicly threatening Israel, by saying that he would "scorch half of Israel." The reference was obviously to the use of chemical weapons.

Alarmed at Saddam's intentions, the DIA and US Commands by April 1990 began to monitor Iraqi military activities.[13] In early May 1990, Saddam was warned by a friendly Head of State that there was a "re-thinking" evident in the US attitude towards him. "Saddam was warned that a decision had been taken at the highest level in the West to treat Iraq as a new danger in the region. According to the same source, the West was waiting for an opportunity to remove him from power.[14]

Nearer the Kuwait invasion, on July 17, 1990, the intelligence community first received unconfirmed reports of troop movements and build-up in southern Iraq. Two days later, on July 19, the Defence Intelligence Officer for the Middle East sent a message to Chairman, Joint Chiefs of Staff, that Iraqi military activity near the Kuwaiti border was "not a rehearsal." As early as July 20, the Kuwaitis began to receive CENTCOM data on Iraq. On the same day, Kuwait put its troops on "alert." The CIA Director, William Webster, showed Bush satellite photographs of Iraqi troops massed near the Kuwaiti border and briefed him in considerable detail. These forecasts and briefings evoked little interest.[15] The *Washington Post* of July 20, 1990 reported that a foreign military attaché driving from Baghdad to Kuwait saw hundreds of trucks filled with troops moving south. He estimated that two divisions of the Iraqi army were on the move. The *Post* further reported that this prompted the US to put this area under special satellite surveillance. On August 1, the CIA told the NSC Middle East staff, "this is your final warning."[16] The US Administration could not have been unaware of what was happening and in spite of having prior knowledge decided not to take any action. Nor was any move made for taking preventive action, either by the US or any other international body such as the UN Security Council. In fact even the UN Secretary-General did nothing.

Were the Kuwaitis taken by surprise? Not if you look at the information they received and the way they were reacting. In addition to direct US warnings, the Kuwaitis themselves were receiving sufficient and precise information. A Kuwaiti diplomat stationed in Baghdad sent back several reports of impending Iraqi aggression. His last report was so precise that it pinpointed the exact time and date of the Iraqi attack.[17] After the war, when he tried to highlight this fact by means of a press conference, a Kuwaiti Minister and several Army officers broke up the conference.[18] The Kuwaiti Military Attaché at Basra, Col. Said Mater, informed the Kuwaiti government, well in advance, that the Iraqi attack would commence on August 2! He clarified that he had received this information directly from Iraqi Republican Guard officers. The inescapable conclusion can only be that the Kuwaitis knew perfectly well in advance that Iraq was going to invade.

What about the Iraqis? As had been the practice in the past, did Saddam not cross-check with his "mentors" before launching the attack on Kuwait? After the war, many years later, Saddam's interpreter Sa'adounal-Zubeidi was emphatic. He was quoted as saying in an interview, "I was present at all the three meetings between Saddam and the then US Ambassador April Glaspie during her three-year term. I can say with certainty that the US was in fact notified of the intention to attack Kuwait and responded with acquiescence." On the other hand what were the public signals being sent to Saddam? The signals coming from the US Administration overtly seemed to point in one direction only.

On January 19, 1990, President Bush voided a Congressional prohibition on new Export-Import Bank financing for Iraq. In April 1990, a US Senate delegation led by the then Senate Minority leader Robert Dole assured Saddam Hussein that they on behalf of the President "dissociated" themselves from a VOA broadcast critical of Iraq's human rights record. Dole emphasised that they would oppose any Congressional move to impose "economic sanctions." Also in April 1990, the White House objected to any limitations on the sale of sensitive technology to Iraq and also resisted any attempt to cut "intelligence sharing." On April 25, 1990, Secretary of State Baker most unusually refused to criticise Saddam when the latter said that Iraq would use chemical weapons to deter a nuclear attack from Israel.

On July 24, 1990, just six days prior to the Kuwaiti invasion, Margaret Tutwiler, the US State Department spokeswoman, said "We do not have any defence treaties with Kuwait. There are no special defence or security commitments to Kuwait."[19] However, a most important and a crucial meeting took place on July 25, 1990 between Saddam Hussein and the US Ambassador to Iraq, April Glaspie. Saddam began the meeting by complaining about Kuwait. He referred to the fact that apart from Kuwait "stealing" Iraqi oil from the Rumaila oilfield, it was producing far over its allotted OPEC quota. Under OPEC rules in force at that time, Kuwait had a production quota of 1.5 mb/d. It was reportedly producing about 2.4 mb/d (some say 1.9mb/d). The upshot was that oil prices crashed from the OPEC favoured US$18 per barrel to US$ 14 per barrel. Saddam remonstrated that this meant that Iraq was losing US$ 1 billion per year from every drop of US$ 1 from the price set by OPEC. Saddam estimated that in all Iraq had lost about US$ 14 billion. No one disputed the overproduction figures. Ambassador Glaspie responded to Saddam as follows:

> We have no opinion on Arab-Arab conflicts, like your border disagreement with Kuwait. I was in the US embassy in Kuwait during the late 60s. The instruction we had during this period was that we should express no opinion on this issue and that the issue is not associated with America. James Baker has directed our official spokesman to emphasise this instruction. We hope you can solve this problem using any suitable methods via Klibi or via Mubarak. All that we hope is that these issues are solved quickly.(Transcript released by Iraq). Nevertheless the US still believed that Saddam was "their man."[20]

If Saddam had any lingering doubts about the attitude of the US, these were soon cleared. Kevin Phillips writes in his book *AmericanDynasty* that on July 28, 1990 just two days before the invasion, the then CIA Director told President Bush that Iraq intended to invade Kuwait, but would confine itself to annexing the Kuwaiti islands of Bubiyan and Warba as also some part of the Rumaila oilfields. There was no reaction from Bush.[21] On the eve of the invasion, on July 31, 1990, US Assistant Secretary of State Kelly told the House Foreign Affairs Sub-Committee, "We have no position on border disputes in the area." Pressed if the US had treaty commitments to defend Kuwait, Kelly said an emphatic "No!" The signals from the US to Saddam right till the end could not have been clearer.[22] There was no warning to Saddam to desist from invading Kuwait. There was no show of force. It could have been so easily done, as the British did when the then Iraqi President Qasim had threatened to invade Kuwait. He hastily withdrew all threats of invasion after the British warned him.

Following the Iraqi invasion and occupation of Kuwait, the UN Security Council at its 2933rd meeting on August 6, 1990 adopted Resolution 661. This Resolution, under Chapter VII, was adopted by 13 votes to none with two abstentions (Cuba and Yemen). The UNSC imposed stringent economic sanctions that also involved a full trade embargo. Foreign assets of Iraq were also largely frozen. Iraq thus became the sixteenth country to suffer such ignominy. Even this action by the UN Security Council was a stand-alone action. In June and August 1980 the UN Security Council declared Israel's annexation of Jerusalem as "null and void" under international law. In December 1981 the UN Security Council declared Israel's annexation of the Syrian Golan Heights also as "null and void" under international law. But curiously nothing has been heard since and no action has been taken to restore status quo ante. The reasons are obvious.

Over the next few months, the UNSC passed a series of resolutions, each getting steadily stronger in content. Mandatory economic sanctions were imposed on Iraq. As nothing seemed to succeed before Iraqi obduracy, the UNSC passed Resolution 678 demanding that Iraq withdraw from Kuwait by January 15, 1991 and if Iraq did not comply, Resolution 678 authorised member states to use "all necessary means, including force" to evict Iraqi forces from Kuwait. The UNSC vote was not unanimous. Cuba and Yemen voted against the resolution. As Secretary of State Baker reportedly remarked of the Yemeni

Ambassador, "I hope he enjoyed the applause because this will turn out to be the most expensive vote he ever cast." Three days later the US cut its entire US$ 70 million aid budget to Yemen! Other non-permanent members of the UNSC such as Zaire, Ethiopia and Colombia received both blandishments and threats. They were offered low cost oil and the resumption of military aid suspended as a result of human rights violations. They had little choice. The Soviets too sided with the US and were apparently "helped" to take a favourable decision on receiving a soft loan from Kuwait amounting to US$ 300 million and US$ 3 billion from the Saudis.

It is to the credit of President Bush that he did give a final warning to Saddam. In a letter addressed to Saddam on January 9, 1991 Bush "warned" Saddam as follows:

> It is said by some that you do not understand just how isolated Iraq is and what Iraq faces as a result ... but unless you withdraw from Kuwait completely and without condition, you will lose more than Kuwait ... the choice is yours to make. What is at stake demands that no opportunity be lost to avoid a certain calamity for the people of Iraq ... Iraq is already feeling the sanctions mandated by the UN. Should war come, it would be a far greater tragedy for you and your country ... I write this letter not to threaten, but to inform.

Saddam never heeded President Bush's warning and was unceremoniously ousted from Kuwait by western military action on behalf of the UN. But why did preventive diplomacy fail?

One of the most significant factors was the misperceptions on the part of the Iraqi leadership. Iraq did not understand the radical political changes in the Soviet Union and in US-Soviet relations. The Iraqi leadership did not understand US domestic politics. They also underestimated President Bush's need to improve his popularity ratings and the Iraqi leadership overestimated their own ability to amass popular Arab support, and overestimated Arab unwillingness to accept US intervention and troops.

Another significant factor was the misperceptions and mixed signals from the international community. Arab states sent ambiguous signals, perhaps waiting to see the eventual outcome. The UN's contribution to preventative diplomacy was too little, too late. The UN showed little interest in the initial dispute, even after Iraqi troops began massing on the Kuwaiti border. UN member states also failed to bring the issue before the Security Council. The UN Secretary-General failed to exercise his broad discretion, and neither discussed the issue with the parties, nor brought it before the Security Council. The Secretary-General could have done so under Article 99 of the UN Charter.

Regional organisations did not do much preventative diplomacy either. The Gulf Cooperation Countries did not stir at all. The Arab League did not pursue mediation, though its charter authorises it to mediate any dispute which threatens to lead to war. They were perhaps all waiting for the US to act.[23]

On August 6, 1990, the UN Security Council had imposed economic sanctions on Iraq, prohibiting all imports (except medical supplies) and exports, unless the Security Council permitted exceptions. While the sanctions were intended to limit Iraq's access to weapons materials, the overall effect on the Iraqi people was devastating, as figures below show:

- 23 per cent of all births affected by low infant birth weight
- 1 in 4 children under 5 years old affected by chronic malnutrition—double the amount from 1991 to 1996
- Only 41 per cent of the population had regular access to clean water
- 83 per cent of schools in Central and Southern Iraq needed substantial repairs
- School enrolment declined to 53 per cent

Source: "Guide to Sanctions" (based on UN Security Council Humanitaria)

The UN Security Council however did respond by passing Resolutions 706 and 712. These resolutions did permit Iraq to make emergency oil sales, but only for US$ 1.6 billion over a six-month period. This was not only to fund humanitarian supplies, but also to fund compensation claims, weapons inspections, demarcating the boundary with Kuwait and other UN expenses. In total the amount available for Iraqi humanitarian needs was estimated at only US$ 930 million! Even the UN Secretary-General suggested that the amount should be increased to US$ 2.4 billion, but the Security Council rejected this suggestion. What the UN Security Council now suggested would not have met even half of what was suggested by the Aga Khan report. Even if the UNSC recommendations were accepted, the desperate situation of the Iraqi people would have continued and there was every chance that it would not have made any material difference. In addition, there were a number of unnecessary features that proved too much for the Iraqi government to accept. It was quite obvious that they were designed to humiliate the Iraqi government, more than provide relief under a legitimate humanitarian relief programme.

Some of the features were that all revenue from Iraqi oil sales was to be put into a UN "escrow account." Secondly, humanitarian purchases were to be screened and approved by the "Sanctions Committee" under the Security Council and subject to UN monitoring and supervision inside Iraq. Thirdly, as all the money was to be under UN control and all goods to be purchased were to be monitored by the UN, it is difficult to explain the necessity of putting an upper limit on the quantity of oil to be sold other than as a political motive. The motive obviously was to make the sanctions bite hard and as much as possible. It was obvious that by linking the humanitarian aspects with compensation for payments for weapons inspections and the Iraq-Kuwait boundary, the whole issue was politicised.

Despite the acknowledged deprivations of the Iraqi people, it was clear that they would not receive any major assistance unless their government agreed to "political conditions" attached. After almost a year spent in negotiations, the Iraqi government turned down the offer, as the conditions were far too humiliating. In the meanwhile, the pathetic condition of the Iraqi population continued to deteriorate. The evidence was all too apparent. Infant mortality rates were probably the highest in the Arab world and health care levels were far below pre-war levels. A team of lawyers and health care specialists from Harvard visited 46 hospitals and twenty-eight water sewage facilities and found death amongst children less than five years of age had quintupled and that almost a million were starving. Later, the UNICEF estimated that about 4,500 children under five were dying every month from hunger and disease.

Thus a strange situation prevailed. On the one hand the UN Security Council led by the western powers would not "lift" the sanctions against Iraq till a regime change had taken place and on the other hand other UN agencies such as UNICEF, WFP, FAO, WHO, UNDP and other humanitarian agencies were involved in lessening the ill-effects of the sanctions against civilian Iraqi population. The harsher the UNSC sanctions became, the greater the effort that UN humanitarian agencies had to put to save the people of Iraq from their suffering. Nevertheless, despite the best efforts of the western powers Saddam could not be toppled. The UNSC sanctions regime only tended to strengthen his internal position.

The Second Gulf War (2003)

As the years progressed it was clear that Saddam could not be toppled either by UN sponsored sanctions or by internal dissent. In fact he seemed to be getting stronger by the day and it was obvious that most countries were now weary of continuing sanctions against Iraq. It was only a matter of time before they would have to be lifted. Correspondingly the anxiety levels of the western powers also increased for they were keen to tap Iraq's vast oil resources. Saddam seemed to stand in the way.

Speaking in London at the London Institute of Petroleum in 1999 the soon to be the Vice-President of the US, Dick Cheney made the following assertion:

> By some estimates there will be an average of 2 per cent annual growth in global oil demand over the years ahead

> along with conservatively a 3 per cent natural decline in production from existing reserves. That means by 2010 we will need on the order of an additional 50 million barrels a day. So where is the oil going to come from? Governments and the national oil companies are obviously in control of about 90 per cent of the assets. *Oil remains fundamentally a government business. While many regions of the world offer great oil opportunities, the Middle East with two thirds of the world's oil and the lowest cost, is still where the prize ultimately lies* ... (emphasis added).

As the new century dawned George Bush and Dick Cheney assumed office in Washington, along with Donald Rumsfeld as the new Secretary for Defence. These were the years that the neo-cons were in the ascendant in Washington. The neo-cons firmly promoted policies that advocated US military "activism" to the point of using overwhelming "force" to secure US strategic goals in the Middle East. Included in this was the belief that the US must effectively "demonstrate" its overwhelming military and economic superiority. To maintain such a policy it would be imperative to "secure" the oilfields of the Middle East, particularly those of Iraq, for without secure supplies of oil, no major power projection could be sustained. By overthrowing Saddam it would also mean the completion of "the job," left half done earlier. Also any threat to Israel, even if it was remote, had to be neutralised. It was to be the new American dominated century! But why single out Iraq and why is Iraqi oil so important?

Of the four major countries in the Arab World, Iraq is the only country that has huge oil assets, a sizeable population and sufficient water resources for sustainable agriculture. Egypt has the river Nile; is overpopulated and has no substantial exportable surplus in oil. Saudi Arabia has huge quantities of oil but no water resources, nor an indigenous population sufficient to feed its great power ambitions. Syria is bereft of both.

As for Iraq its massive oil wealth has been both a boon as well as its nemesis. Usually three reasons are advanced for this. Firstly, Iraq's oil is of very high quality and has attractive chemical properties such as high carbon content, lightness and low sulphur content that make it especially suitable for refining for high-value products. For this reason Iraqi oil commands a high premium in the oil market. Secondly, Iraq's oil is plentiful. Its proven reserves are estimated at 115 billion barrels.[24] There are many promising areas in Iraq that still remain unexplored. The US Energy Department has estimated Iraqi reserves at 400 billion barrels. Pre-US Invasion, oil was being pumped out of only 15 of the proven 74 oil wells. Thus even with present estimated reserves, Iraq's oil reserves are the second largest in the world, constituting some 11 per cent of the world's total. These reserves are equal to those of the US, Canada, Mexico, Western Europe, Australia and New Zealand combined. By any account Iraq's oil reserves are huge! Thirdly, the costs of producing oil in Iraq are probably the lowest in the world. More than a third of Iraq's oil lies in wells that are just 600 metres from the surface. They can be tapped relatively easily. It costs about US$ 1.5 or about a dollar per barrel to produce oil in Iraq, as against US $5 in countries such as Malaysia and Oman. (Year 2000 prices.) In countries such as Mexico and Russia, the costs are significantly higher. Offshore production areas like the North Sea with expensive platforms can cost even much more. In Texas and other North American areas production costs are also prohibitively expensive. This is of course subject to security concerns being met. Combined with its water resources, is it any wonder that the land between the Euphrates and the Tigris has been coveted by many throughout the centuries.

On August 15, 2002 Brent Scowcroft, the former National Security Advisor to the elder Bush, wrote a very perceptive piece in the *Wall Street Journal* which was seen by many as the sage advice of the father (the first President Bush) to the son, President George W. Bush. Advising against intervention in Iraq, Scowcroft wrote that:

> ...this would divert for some indefinite period from our war on terrorism and that any military campaign would have to be followed by large-scale long-term military occupation.

The then policymakers in the US did not pay heed to Brent Scowcroft's words of wisdom with disastrous consequences, both for the US as well as for the hapless people of Iraq. The US-led invasion forces claimed to be acting under UN resolutions, although they had failed to obtain a clear and specific UN Security Council resolution authorising military action. Occupation is never easy even if it is disguised as "liberation," no matter how odious the former rulers are. No one seriously doubted that Saddam would be easily overthrown. The question really was, what do you do afterwards? And what have been the results in the last ten years?

When the US decided to pull out in December 2011, it had suffered about 4,500 dead and 25,000 soldiers injured. About 100,000 Iraqis had died and 1.5 million had fled abroad and about 1.7 million were internally displaced. The US has spent over a trillion and a half dollars and this huge expenditure has nearly unhinged its domestic economic equilibrium. The US is still counting the costs of its foreign military adventure.

Strategically, the results for the US have been even more disconcerting. With the overthrow of the Sunni-led Saddam government it was a foregone conclusion that any future dispensation would of necessity have a large Shiite component. This is because the Shiites are the largest community in Iraq and in any democratic set-up, they were bound to win, even though voting has largely been on tribal and sectarian lines. The shrewd Shiite clerics based near the holy cities of Najaf and Karbala, waited for their opportunity and watched with obvious satisfaction while the US got rid of Saddam and his Sunni-dominated government (they failed to do so during the Iran-Iraq War 1980-88). They realised that the Sunni leadership was bound to get decimated at the hands of the US and they knew that the time would soon arrive for the clerical leadership of the Shiites to play the dominant role. The Shiites seminaries in Iraq have close links with their fellow Shiites in Iran. These ties are most evident in the network of ayatollahs, their representatives and organisations. The British and before them the Ottomans feared such links and therefore always encouraged Sunni domination of Iraq's political space. All rulers of Iraq right up to Saddam were Sunnis.

With the Sunni leadership decimated it was but natural that a Shiite-led government would take its place. This Shiite led government not only refused to let US troops stay on in Iraq, but has been fairly active in supporting its fellow Shiites in Syria. That Iran has utilised the space provided by Iraq to reinforce its alliance with Assad of Syria is there for all to see. Politically, the Sunni Arab bloc led by Saudi Arabia, Jordan and the Gulf States finds itself in a bind for there is no Iraq to bolster their strength as in the past. Iraq would pride itself as the eastern gateway of the Arabs (al-bawwabeh al-sharqiyah), the cradle of Arab civilisation and had always played a major role in Arab affairs. The loss of Iraq to the Sunni Arab leadership is indeed a tipping point in the history of Inter-Arab relations. Conversely, the strategic gain for Iran has been enormous.

Iraq is yet another example of how one Super-power acting on its own freed the issue and the prospects of international community acting or preventive diplomacy operating were rather remote.

CASE STUDY—LIBYA

On December 17, 2010 when an ordinary street vendor in Tunisia set himself on fire, little did he realise that he would in effect be setting the Arab Street alight. Soon the conflagration spread from one Arab country to another and long-time dictators like Mubarak of Egypt fell by the wayside. Gaddafi of Libya too did not escape the raging fire. In recent times the Arab experience has not been particularly forthcoming. Much of the Arab world is ruled by hereditary monarchies, military regimes and autocrats. A recent trend has been that even autocracies have become hereditary, as in the case of Syria. There is hardly any functioning democracy anywhere. This is particularly so in oil rich Arab countries. Even where democratic elections were held, the inconvenient winners were soon overthrown or not allowed to assume power due to significant external intervention or with the connivance of multinational oil companies, as in the case of Algeria. In most Arab countries there is no tradition of democracy. In the case of Libya, there has never been such a tradition for it is still a feudal and a tribal society. It has a small population living mainly along the coastal areas that can easily fracture into warring tribal affiliations, once a firm hand is removed.

Although the issue of Libyan support for terrorism had abated somewhat since 2003, there was of course not much to commend the Gaddafi regime as regards its human rights record. The Gaddafi regime was one of the more odious Arab regimes whose flair for initiating terrorism and terror-related acts is perhaps rather well known. The Lockerbie bombing of Pan Am Flight 103 over Scotland in 1988 and several other initiatives the Gaddafi regime undertook, including encouraging nuclear proliferation, are well-documented. Libya came under partial UN sanctions in March 1992 in an attempt to force it to surrender two of its citizens wanted in connection with the Lockerbie bombing. The sanctions were not comprehensive and involved only an arms embargo and a ban on the supply and sale of aircraft. In November 1993 they were further tightened but excluded the sale of oil. Eventually there was an agreement with the Libyan government and the two suspects were handed over. However sanctions were not lifted till much later, but there is no doubt sanctions had played a role.

The clandestine nuclear activities of some Pakistani nuclear scientists, now in the open, revealed that they were substantial beneficiaries of the Gaddafi largesse. It was only under intense international pressure in 2004 that Libya agreed to abandon its WMD programmes and also agreed to comply with the provisions of the NPT. This decision was welcomed by the western powers at that time and it was seen by them as a vindication of the US-led invasion of Iraq. They felt that the fear of an external intervention had indeed induced Gaddafi to give up his quest for WMD. Nevertheless, the Gaddafi regime did not desist from financing acts of terrorism, including trying to meddle in Kashmir on behalf of Pakistan, where it financed a "study" sponsored by Chatham House to conduct a so-called "survey" of Kashmiri opinion.

It is indeed interesting to examine the role played by the UN when the Arab street protests first surfaced in Libya or were induced from the outside as alleged by some. The

Libyan Chargé d'Affaires to the United Nations, Ibrahim Dabbashi took the unusual action of first announcing to the press that he had *defected* from the government of Libya at the UN. He then requested for an emergency meeting of the Security Council on the situation in Libya. At a press conference, he claimed that Libyan government troops had used "brutal tactics" to suppress the demonstrators and that Libyan government war planes had "fired-on" them at Tripoli. He however offered no proof to support his assertion.[1] He called for the overthrow of the Libyan government headed by Muammar Gaddafi.

Ibrahim Dabbashi, now a former official of the Libyan UN Mission and who no longer represented the government of Libya, then sent a letter dated February 21, 2011 to the Security Council. The letter states as follows:

> In accordance with rule 3 of the provisional rules of procedure of the Security Council, I have the honour to request an urgent meeting of the Council, to discuss the grave situation in Libya and to take the appropriate actions.

Not unsurprisingly, Dabbashi's letter was given official document identification number S/2011/102, dated February 22, 2011 and listed as a Security Council document. It is worth noting that Rule 3 of the Security Council's Provisional Rules of Procedure *provides for a member nation of the United Nations to request a meeting.*[2] A simple reading of Rule 3 would make it obvious that Dabbashi, a defector from the Libyan Mission to the UN, was not entitled to request for any Security Council meeting and that too request the UN Security Council to take punitive action against the government he had defected from and which continued to be a member of the UN![3]

On the next working day on February 22, 2011, the Security Council held a closed meeting on the situation in Libya, under the title "Peace and Security in Africa—Libya."[4] At the meeting the Security Council heard a report on developments in Libya from Lynn Pascoe, the Under Secretary-General for Political Affairs at the UN. Later at a meeting with members of the press, Lynn Pascoe when asked if he had any evidence of atrocities in Tripoli responded that the UN people on the ground there had no such direct evidence.[5]

The Libyan Ambassador to the UN, Abdel Rahman Shalgham also attended the February 22, Security Council meeting and in informal comments after the meeting, indicated that he had been in contact with Tripoli and was told that the alleged "atrocities" that the media was claiming were not true. Similarly, speaking to the press, he indicated that he had been in contact with government officials in Tripoli who said that they, too, disputed the claims of atrocities taking place in Tripoli and planned to invite journalists from Al Arabiya and CNN to see for themselves that the allegations were inaccurate.[6]

The Reuters News Agency described the February 22, closed meeting of the Security Council as follows:

> UNITED NATIONS | Tuesday, February 22, 2011 4:42 pm GMT (Reuters)—The UN Security Council held closed-door discussions on Tuesday on the crisis in Libya, with Western envoys and Libya's own breakaway delegation calling for action by the 15-nation body …

> The Council met at the request of Libyan Deputy Ambassador Ibrahim Dabbashi, who along with most other staff at Libya's UN mission announced on Monday they were no longer working for leader Muammar Gaddafi and represented the country's people. They called for Gaddafi's overthrow.

Meanwhile pressure on the Security Council was also building to take some action to prevent further bloodshed. On February 25, 2011, the UN Human Rights Council strongly condemned "the gross and systematic human rights violations committed in Libya, including indiscriminate armed attacks against civilians, extrajudicial killings, arbitrary arrests, detention and torture of peaceful demonstrators, some of which may also amount to crimes against humanity." It established an independent international commission of inquiry to investigate the alleged human rights violations, and recommended to the UN General Assembly to suspend Libya's membership of the Human Rights Council. The General Assembly did so on March 1, 2011. The Committee of Permanent Representatives to the Organisation of the Islamic Conference endorsed this statement.[7] The Peace and Security Council of the African Union also strongly condemned the "indiscriminate and excessive use of force and lethal weapons against peaceful protesters, in violation of human rights and international Humanitarian Law."[8] Furthermore, the Council called the aspirations of the Libyan people for democracy and political reform "legitimate." The African Commission on Human and Peoples' Rights condemned the violence and use of force against civilians and the suppression of peaceful demonstrators, and called on the government of Libya to immediately end the violence and to ensure the respect for human rights in Libya. Others, including the Gulf Cooperation Council also voiced their deep apprehensions over the turn of events in Libya.[9]

Then on February 25, the Libyan Ambassador to the UN, Abdel Rahman Shalgham, a former Foreign Minister of Libya, announced his defection. The President of the Security Council under Rule 37 of the Security Council's Provisional Rules of Procedure invited the defecting Ambassador to take part in the meeting. If Rule 37 is examined it would be obvious that *only a member nation can be invited to participate. A defecting Ambassador or diplomat cannot take part in a UN Security Council meeting* (emphasis added). This Rule applies *to an official representative* of a member nation of the UN and not to someone who no longer represents that nation by his own admission. A simple reading of Rule 37 would confirm this position:

> [Rule 37]: Any Member of the United Nations which is not a member of the Security Council may be invited, as the result of a decision of the Security Council, to participate, without vote, in the discussion of any question brought before the Security Council when the Security Council considers that the interests of that Member are specially affected, or when a Member brings a matter to the attention of the Security Council in accordance with Article 35 (1) of the Charter.

At the Security Council meeting on February 25, the role of the UN Secretary-General Ban Ki-moon was even more intriguing. He spoke to the Security Council about the situation in Cote d'Ivoire and Libya. In his remarks on Libya, the Secretary-General claimed that he was basing his reports on accounts from "the press, human rights groups and civilians on the ground." He acknowledged that there was no conclusive proof for his allegations, but dismissed this lack of verifiable information by saying *that action should be taken along with efforts to get more reliable information* (emphasis added). This proposal of the UN Secretary-General was clearly one-sided, for he not only admitted that he had no verifiable information, but if he was truly impartial he should have insisted that at the very least an enquiry must be held first before any conclusions could be drawn. This is one of the recommendations made by Ban Ki-moon himself elsewhere!

After the Secretary-General presented his unverified allegations, the former Libyan Ambassador was asked to take the floor. Former Ambassador Shalgham as expected made a virulent denunciation of the Gaddafi government, comparing Gaddfi to Hitler. Shalgham presented no proof for his allegations, nor was he asked to present any. Instead, he was consoled by the Secretary-General and members of the Security Council, with several Security Council members, embracing and comforting him.[10]

The following day, Saturday, February 26, a day-long emergency meeting was held at the Security Council. While the Security Council was discussing a resolution about Libya, Shalgham is reported to have sent a letter to the Security Council to influence the votes of its members. One journalist offered the following as the content of the letter former Ambassador Shalgham sent to the Security Council:

> With reference to the Draft Resolution on Libya before the Security Council, I have the honour to confirm that the Libyan Delegation to the United Nations supports the measures proposed in the draft resolution to hold to account those responsible for the armed attacks against the Libyan Civilians, including trough [sic] the International Criminal Court.

On February 26, 2011 the UN Security Council passed Resolution 1970.[11] In the preamble paragraphs of the resolution, the Security Council referred to the statements and condemnations made by other organs of the United Nations as well as by regional organisations. Elaborating on the alleged human rights violations, the Security Council expressed its concern at the situation in Libya and condemned the violence and the use of force before it deplored more specifically the gross and systematic violation of human rights and the incitement to hostility and violence against the civilian population *made from the highest level of the Libyan government*. The reference to the "highest levels" of government was undoubtedly aimed at the Libyan leader, Gaddafi.

The UN Security Council did not have any independent analysis of the situation before it nor did it seek any for evaluating the situation. The UN Security Council simply continued to stipulate that the "widespread and systematic attacks currently taking place in the Libyan Arab Jamahiriya against the civilian population may amount to crimes against humanity." Without explicitly determining the existence of a threat to the peace under Article 39, the Security Council concluded that it had authority to act under Chapter VII and took measures under Article 41. It demanded an immediate end to the violence and called upon Libya to respect its obligations under human rights law and international humanitarian law. Furthermore, it referred the situation in Libya to the International Criminal Court, and it imposed sanctions on the Gaddafi regime, including an arms embargo, a travel ban, and an asset freeze. According to journalists waiting outside the Security Council meeting on February 26, some Security Council members indicated that their aim was to induce more defections of Libyan officials by including referrals to the International Criminal Court (ICC) in the Security Council resolution they were proposing. This amounts to using the ICC as a political tool rather than as a means of punishing actual crimes.

Libya acceded to the International Convention on Civil and Political Rights in May 1970. It ratified the African Charter on Human Rights and People's Rights in June 1987. Although it ratified the Convention against Torture in May 1989, it is not a member of the Treaty creating the ICC. It has neither signed nor ratified the Rome Statute of the ICC. Thus in the case of Libya only international law is applicable. Though the UN Charter provides for the Security Council to create tribunals it has no provision to force a nation not a member of a treaty organisation creating a tribunal to be subject to its jurisdiction. When Security Council members are asked under what authority they refer a national of a state not a member of the ICC to its jurisdiction, they cite a provision in the ICC treaty. But a provision of the ICC treaty cannot be substituted for some provision of the UN Charter. No provision of the UN Charter has been cited as providing the authority for the Security Council referrals of non-treaty members to the jurisdiction of the ICC.

The Secretary-General spoke in the UN Security Council and welcomed the sanctions and saw them as a means for a new governance regime in Libya. He said:

> The sanctions that the Council has imposed are a necessary step to speed the transition to a new system of governance that will have the consent and participation of the people.

It is not for the Secretary-General to determine what form of government a member of the UN should have!

This sequence of events can only be seen as a violation of the Security Council's obligations under the UN charter. The provision of the Security Council rules used to invite the defecting former Libyan government officials into Security Council meetings were provisions providing for officials representing the government of Libya to speak. The defecting officials were now former government officials and as such had no authority to speak for the official government of Libya, and no authority to appear at Security Council meetings as officials of Libya.[12]

The actions of such officials were not the actions of a member government. Unspoken was the process of how they had defected and through what arrangements with US and other western government agencies they had gained the ability to remain in the US and to participate in Security Council procedures. The Security Council was providing support and aid to members of a group attempting to carry out a coup against the government of Libya. Such an action is contrary to the obligations of the UN Charter requiring the non-intervention in the affairs of member nations.

The Security Council supported these defectors acting to overthrow the government of Libya. Also it failed to make any effort to initiate an independent investigation of what was happening in Libya. Apart from the biased western or Qatar supported media reports (reports from Al Jazeera only represented the Libyan opposition viewpoint when it reported on the Libyan conflict), the Security Council did not seek out any other source of information. UN personnel in Libya were not requested to investigate the allegations.

No legitimate Libyan government official was invited to take part in Security Council proceedings. When the Libyan government tried to appoint legitimate government officials to replace the defector delegation, the US government would not approve the visa requests for the replacement delegates, in violation of the Host Country obligations of the US. In this way, the US prevented the Libyan government from being able to present its case before the Security Council.

By March 3, 2011, the Spokesman for the Secretary-General acknowledged that the Secretary-General had received notice from the Libyan government withdrawing the credentials of Dabbashi and Shalgham.[13] Yet for a period of time, they had continued to speak to reporters at the official Security Council stake-out and their statements to the press were covered by the UN media services and were treated as official Libyan government statements available at the UN Security Council website. Eventually the access of the two diplomats was converted from diplomatic passes into courtesy passes granted at the discretion of the Secretariat so they could continue to have access to the UN, but on a more restricted basis than the official diplomatic access. When some journalists questioned the grounds on which these defector diplomats continued to have access to official UN and Security Council procedures, such as, requesting a meeting of the Security Council, the spokesman for the Secretary-General said that someone who has presented credentials to the Secretary-General is the representative of a nation.[14]

Disagreeing with the Spokesman's response, one journalist pointed out that the "Request for a meeting of the Security Council normally is by request from Member States, not from Ambassadors sitting in missions. Ambassadors ask for a meeting of the Council on the basis of a letter from the Foreign Ministry and, in this case, presumably there is no such letter emanating from the Foreign Ministry of Libya. So, on what basis, legal basis, is the Security Council meeting?" Instead of acknowledging the accuracy of the explanation that it is member nations that are represented at the Security Council, not an Ambassador, particularly not an Ambassador who has defected, the Spokesperson for the Secretary-General answered: "I think you know what I am going to say ... ask the Security Council."

The Security Council should have found a way to hear from a member of the government of Libya, rather than substituting a defector Ambassador and his delegation for the official delegation of Libya. Despite several efforts of the government of Libya to appoint a new Ambassador to replace the defector Ambassador and his staff members who had defected, neither the UN nor the US, the host country of the UN, acted in accord with their obligations to make this possible.

A letter from the Libyan government dated March 17, was sent to the Security Council President. It appears that this letter was not made an official document of the Security Council. Yet this letter provided the Libyan government explanation of what was happening. According to Article 32 of the UN Charter, the Security Council has an obligation to hear from member nations. The relevant portion of Article 32 states: "Any member of the United Nations which is not a member of the Security Council ... if it is a party to a dispute under consideration by the Security Council, shall be invited to participate, without vote, in the discussion relating to that dispute."[15]

This would be true as well, for a state which is not a Member of the United Nations.

The picture the Libyan government presents in the communication to the Security Council is one where there is an armed confrontation between armed insurgents and the State Authorities.[16]

This is a different description of the situation than any of the members of the Security Council publicly considered on February 26 when the Security Council passed Resolution 1970, or on March 17 when it passed Resolution 1973.[17]

Shortly after the intervention started, the intervening states more openly acknowledged that regime change was, in fact, the final objective of the military operation. In an open letter dated April 15, 2011, US President Barack Obama, French President Nicolas Sarkozy, and UK Prime Minister David Cameron, while emphasising that their duty and mandate under Resolution 1973 was not to remove Gaddafi by force, held that "it is impossible to imagine a future for Libya with Gaddafi in power" and that it is "unthinkable that someone who has tried to massacre his own people can play a part in their future government." The Group of Eight met at a summit in France on May 26 and 27 and issued a final communiqué that, in surprisingly clear terms, *emphasised that regime change was the ultimate goal of the international community's efforts in Libya: "Gaddafi and the Libyan government have failed to fulfil their responsibility to protect the Libyan population and have lost all legitimacy. He has no future in a free, democratic Libya. He must go.*" (Emphasis added.)

In the letter of March 17, Libya explains that what is happening is a confrontation between terrorist groups and the State Authorities. It cites Libyan Law No. 38 of 1974, Article 1, as the basis for the armed forces of Libya to "maintain security, if the general safety of the 'Republic' or any part of it so requires." The letter explains that "Libyan army camps that have been attacked have taken no violent action against the armed attackers until the latter have brandished their weapons." This is in conformity with Libyan law, the letter notes.

The letter explains that "Article 2 of the same law provides that orders to fire may be given in the following circumstances:

- If any member of forces is attacked.
- If rebels refuse to restore order, after having been warned and given the opportunity to do so.
- If rebels carry out an armed attack against persons or property."

The letter from the Libyan government describes how the government is fulfilling its responsibility to protect Libyan residents and citizens by confronting the armed insurgents.

The letter also says that Resolution 1970 and the draft of Resolution 1973, the resolution being considered for adoption on March 17, and subsequently adopted, "exceed the mandate" of the Security Council.

The letter says that "what is at issue is not a conflict between two States, as provided for in Article 24 of the Charter of the United Nations." The Council therefore has no authority to adopt resolutions in such cases. The Charter, the letter explained, "provides that States shall refrain from the threat or use of force against the territorial integrity of any State."

Also in the letter, Libya referred to the mission to Libya by the African Union that was planned for March 20 to negotiate a political solution. The letter called the adoption of resolutions under Chapter VII premature, until an evaluation of the situation had been made by the African Union.

The Security Council made no mention of the letter or the points it raised when it went ahead and passed Resolution 1973 on the evening of March 17. Only an AP article mentioned that there was such a letter and referred to some of its contents, including the challenge Libya presented to the section of Resolution 1970 referring Gaddafi and his family members to the International Criminal Court (ICC).[18]

After the March 17 Security Council meeting, the US and then NATO began bombing Libya.

A letter dated March 19 from the government of Libya has been made one of the documents of the Security Council. In the letter the Foreign Minister refers to previous letters that he sent to the Security Council which are not found in Security Council records. In the March 19 letter, he writes:[19]

"In my previous letters to you, I emphasised that an external conspiracy was targeting Jamahiriya and its unity and territorial integrity. I pointed out that the Security

Council had been drawn into implementing this conspiracy by its adoption of Resolution 1970 (2011) and 1973 (2011) under which a ban was imposed on all aviation in the airspace of the Libyan Arab Jamahiriya. By taking this decision," the March 19 letter explained, "the Security Council has paved the way for military aggression against Libyan territory. France and the United States have bombarded several civilian sites, thereby violating all international norms and instruments, most notably the Charter of the United Nations, which provides for non-intervention in the affairs of member states."

Libya asked the Security Council to hold an emergency meeting "in order to halt this aggression, the purpose of which is not to protect civilians, as is purported, but rather to strike civilian sites, economic facilities, and sites belonging to the Armed Peoples on Duty." The UN Security Council discussed this request at a meeting on Monday, March 21 and decided not to grant the Libyan government's request.

As of February 21, the Libyan government has been deprived of the ability to have a representative to the UN. In March, when the Libyan government tried to appoint another Ambassador, the US government did not grant a visa.[20]

Instead the defecting diplomats continued to have access to the UN and to use their presence at the UN to attack the legitimate government of Libya.

An article published by Al Ahram, is unusual in that it presents an account of some of the abuse of Security Council procedures that occurred in passing Resolutions 1970 and 1973 against Libya. The article was written by Curtis Doebbler, the American Human Rights lawyer. Doebbler writes[21]

> The West focused its propaganda machinery on the UN with a vengeance. And it was no mere ordinary propaganda campaign but a full-blown orchestration of history for the books. First, Libyan diplomats were induced and threatened to step down from their positions and promised that if they supported the opposition they would be "taken care of." This resulted in the Libyan diplomats at the UN not only resigning, but doing so and still maintaining a type of diplomatic status that allowed them to advocate on behalf of the armed rebels who were challenging the government of Libya for control of their country.

Doebbler continues:

> This was accomplished by the spurious actions of UN Secretary-General Ban Ki-moon, who issued special passes to the former Libyan diplomats after their government had withdrawn their credentials. Bypassing the UN General Assembly's Credentials Committee and well-established protocol, the UN Secretary-General for the first time in the world body's history personally favoured one side in what was by now a civil war.

Among Security Council members there have been a number of complaints that the resolution they allowed to pass (1973) did not authorise the kind of NATO bombing of Libya in support of the rebels that has been carried out. Because of the veto power of the US, France and the UK, the Security Council appears to have no means of oversight over NATO to stop what they believe to be an abuse of Security Council processes.

In the context of the sequence of events that took place at the Security Council in February and March, the question asked at the press conference in April, "... are we to expect a more aggressive and proactive posture on the part of the Security Council in supporting rebel groups?" is about a serious change. The precedent set by the Security Council's supporting an armed insurgency against the government of a UN member nation is a significant and dangerous precedent. It is an important issue to be seriously examined.[22]

The fact that the western powers were determined to pursue a regime change is therefore quite self-evident. The reasons are not far to seek. That the UN Secretariat, headed by the UN Secretary-General, played a partisan role is a matter for concern. According to the International Energy Agency (IEA) Libya, a member of OPEC, has the largest oil reserves in Africa with an annual production of some 1.69 mb/d* of oil (crude and natural gas liquids). Of these volumes, some 1.49 mb/d were exported. Europe receives over 85 per cent of Libya's crude exports, while about 13 per cent heads east of Suez. An additional 0.15 mb/d of crude oil from Libya went to China in 2010, accounting for some 3 per cent of the total Chinese crude imports. One very noticeable fact is that those Western powers that are most active in opposing the Gaddafi regime, namely the US and UK, import only 0.5 per cent and 8.5 per cent respectively of Libyan oil as a percentage of their overall total imports of oil. The inescapable conclusion would be that if the turmoil in Libya were to continue even for any length of time these countries would not face any significant turbulence in their economies. The action initiated by them is for long-term strategic advantages and not any short-term gain. In any case

---

* mb/d: million barrels per day.

Saudi Arabia has promised to make up the shortfall, if any, by increasing its own production.

Although by any standards Libya is not in the league of major oil producers such as Saudi Arabia, Iraq, UAE or for that matter Russia, yet its reserves of crude oil are about 3 per cent of the world's total. Libyan gas reserves are even more important with large areas of the country still to be surveyed. Nevertheless Libyan crude is much in demand. Firstly, it is of very high quality with low sulphur content. Secondly, situated far away from the Gulf region, Libyan oil exports are not subject to the vicissitudes of Gulf region politics. With the threat of a confrontation looming between the West/Israel and Iran over the latter's nuclear ambitions, the control of Libyan oil assets becomes a strategic necessity. The Persian Gulf produces about 27 per cent of the world's oil, while holding about 57 per cent of the total world's crude oil reserves. It also holds about 45 per cent of the total world gas reserves. Any confrontation with Iran will of necessity involve a possible disruption of oil exports through the Straits of Hormuz. It is through this area that the bulk of the West's oil imports pass.

The Western powers were conscious of the strategic utility of Libyan oil reserves. Oil is the engine for economic growth. Oil provides nearly all the energy for transportation, heating for buildings and is the essential feedstock for the plastics, paints, fertiliser and pharmaceutical industries. Oil has a 40 per cent share in the US national energy budget. Modern warfare depends on oil. Virtually all modern weapon systems rely on oil-based fuel, be it tanks, trucks and transportation systems, fighter aircraft or naval vessels. No modern nation can do a power projection abroad if it is not assured of uninterrupted fuel supplies. It is for this reason that governments go to considerable lengths to secure oil supplies. Conversely, it becomes a strategic option if potential adversaries are either denied access to oil production centres or their supply routes are under control. China, a major importer of Libyan oil, thus has cause for worry.

Libya situated just across the Mediterranean Sea is ideally located to supply oil to key European markets without fear of any disruption by political upheavals. In this sense countries situated at the southern rim of Europe are huge beneficiaries. Thus Italy is a major importer of Libyan oil which accounts for 22 per cent of total Italian imports. Similar is the position of countries such as Austria, Greece, Ireland and Spain. With assured supplies available from Libya, Southern Europe becomes less dependent on crude oil and gas supplies from Russia. Libyan gas pipelines under the Mediterranean Sea directly link up with the Southern European grid and to a large extent frees Southern European countries from the politics of oil that Russia practises with other countries, particularly those that once formed a part of the old Soviet Union.

Although India abstained from the UN Security Resolution 1973 that authorised "all necessary" measures to halt what would have been a massacre, it was really a Hobson's choice. It is not easy for newly emerging countries to contemplate intervention in the "internal" affairs of a UN member state. On the other hand, the issue of human rights is very much there and cannot be brushed aside or swept under the carpet. At the same time there were about 20,000 Indians who were living and working in Libya and who would have to be evacuated. They would lose their jobs and means of sustaining a livelihood. Many had family commitments to meet in India on the basis of their earnings in Libya. Many Indian companies had major infrastructure turnkey projects on hand. All would inevitably suffer from the consequences of the conflict in Libya. Similar had been the situation of Indians in Iraq who had had to be evacuated.

Thus as the conflict came to a close with the ouster of Gaddafi, did a democratic form of government evolve in Libya? The Arab experience has not been particularly forthcoming. Much of the Arab world is ruled by hereditary monarchies, military regimes and autocrats. A recent trend has been that even autocracies have become hereditary, as in the case of Syria. There is hardly any functioning democracy anywhere. This is particularly so in oil-rich Arab countries. Even where democratic elections were held, the inconvenient winners were soon overthrown or not allowed to assume power due to significant external intervention or with the connivance of multinational oil companies, as in the case of Algeria. In most Arab countries there is no tradition of democracy. In the case of Libya there has never been such a tradition for it is still a tribal society. It has a small population living mainly along the coastal areas that can easily fracture into warring tribal affiliations. Even if democracy is finally introduced, no matter however fractured, voting patterns will largely be along tribal groupings. Libya will need substantial outside help to foster democracy. Therefore, as elsewhere in oil-rich countries, the role of the multinationals, particularly the oil companies, will be crucial. In the past the role of multinational oil companies has not been very helpful. Looking at the situation from their own perspectives, they have tended to favour an autocratic form of government.

Democracies can sometimes be very stubborn and inconvenient. It is much easier to deal with an autocratic ruler where laws can be enacted or changed at will and without much debate or rancour. A neat "profit-sharing" arrangement has in most cases suited both the ruler and the multinational oil companies. Major oil consuming nations with large economies too do not wish that any disruption is caused in the smooth flow of oil. Most countries would prefer a system that ensures that there is price stability. Any convulsions whether for political or other reasons are not contemplated with any relish. The case of Libya, now that a regime change has been engineered, will be watched with particular attention. Or will one dictator be replaced by another, this time by a convenient one?

CASE STUDY—NORTH KOREA (THE DEMOCRATIC REPUBLIC OF KOREA–DPRK)

The history of the events leading to the Korean War and its aftermath are rather well known and to recount the events would only be repetitive. However it must be remembered that once North Korea had decided to cross the demarcation line in June 1950, the response by the western powers on behalf of South Korea was based on UNSC resolutions. In fact the US and other western powers that actively participated in the fighting were actually doing so under the United Nations banner. When the Chinese government decided to intervene on the side of North Korea to halt the disintegration of the North Korean regime, it did so under the guise of Chinese "People's Volunteers." The People's Republic of China was branded as an "aggressor" by a UNSC resolution and despite China having become a member of the P-5 of the UN Security Council, that resolution branding it as an aggressor still remains on the statute books. Eventually peace was restored on the Korean peninsula on the basis of an armistice signed by North Korea and China on the one side and the US acting on behalf of the UN and South Korea on the other. No peace treaty has yet been signed despite nearly six decades having passed and therefore the belligerents are still technically at war.

During this period of the Korean conflict several "neutral" countries were active in trying to promote peace on the Korean peninsula. One of the countries that was most active was India. Indian diplomats were active with both sides, often travelling to Beijing, Moscow and Washington and New York in order to promote a peaceful settlement. It is said that India did not take the Chinese intervention in Tibet seriously and refused to take up the Tibetan cause in the UN, since it wished to play a greater role on the world stage, particularly in defusing the tension on the Korean peninsula. On November 18, 1950 the US Ambassador at Delhi reported to the US Secretary of State that the then Secretary-General of the External Affairs Ministry Sir Girija Shanker Bajpai told him that India wished to delay "action" on the Tibetan demarches to the UN due to its "efforts in achieving a ceasefire in Korea."[1] Similarly the British were informed that the "timing of the Tibetan appeal needed careful consideration. Korea was obviously of first importance ..."[2]

In more recent times the role of the Non-Aligned countries as well as the UN has taken a back seat and a six-nation dialogue has emerged. This is also because most countries are now able to negotiate directly with each other and therefore do not need interlocutors. These six nations are: China, North Korea, Russia, the US, South Korea and Japan. All six are very heavily involved with the events on the peninsula as their strategic interests are at issue. While both China and Russia have diplomatic relations and resident Embassies in both North and South Korea, neither the US nor the pro-western states of Japan and South Korea have diplomatic relations or resident Embassies in North Korea. A dialogue of sorts, which is both sporadic and subject to the vagaries of politics, exists between the two Korean States. Tension remains high all along the DMZ, with frequent incidents and threats and counter-threats. Often it seems that conflict is imminent, but much of it is bluster, for peace has largely held for the last several decades. None of the principals are interested in a further conflict and that is probably the reason why peace has largely held, despite obvious provocations.

The starting point of the current crisis was the third nuclear test conducted by North Korea in February 2013 and the military exercises conducted jointly by the US and South Korea. These military exercises are conducted regularly by the two countries on an annual basis. However what distinguished them this year was the unusual belligerence shown by the two countries with the US bringing B-52 bombers and B-2 stealth aircraft to South Korea for training purposes. The US made no effort to hide the fact that these aircraft were capable of dropping nuclear bombs. To station nuclear weapons in South Korea, even though in US custody, would presumably be a violation of the NPT since a signatory, South Korea, is barred from possessing nuclear weapons.

The shrill response of North Korea to "Operation Foal Eagle" was expected since the North believes that a major US objective is a "regime change" in North Korea. This belief is fairly widespread in the ruling circles of the North Korean establishment and the US does nothing to encourage them to believe otherwise. The North Koreans have seen what has happened in the case of Libya. Till the time the Libyan leader Gaddafi had an ongoing programme of developing weapons of mass destruction, the western powers did not envisage a policy of "regime change." When he had decided to forgo the development of weapons of mass destruction soon after the US invasion of Iraq, he was at first congratulated for his "far-sighted" policy. Yet when the opportune time came, the western powers had no hesitation in going for a policy of "regime change" knowing full well that Gaddafi had destroyed all his weapons of mass destruction at their behest. The North Korean leadership is conscious of this position. One way to reassure the North Koreans would be to go in for a four-party peace treaty by which North Korea is recognised as a state, particularly by the United States, and for the US to establish diplomatic relations with it.

The secretive regime in North Korea was sharply taken aback when China decided to support UNSC Resolution 2094 which was passed by the Security Council on March 7, 2013. The North Koreans feel that the UN system and its other organs are dominated by the US and therefore its chances of obtaining "justice" are negligible. North Korea was particularly resentful against the Chinese for supporting UNSC 2094 since it contained financial sanctions. Many analysts have interpreted the Chinese leader Xi Jinping's remarks that "no country should be able to throw the region or even the entire world into chaos for selfish gains," as being directed against the North Korean leadership. However that would be reading too much into a relationship that has been forged over decades. There are others who believe that North Korea would do nothing without an explicit clearance from Beijing, considering how closely interlinked the two countries are. That this crisis has shown how dependent the western powers are on China goes without saying and therefore if any country benefits from this crisis, it is China. The North Koreans know that the UN Secretary-General is a former South Korean diplomat and therefore hardly likely to take a benevolent view of their position and in any case the North Koreans are not enamoured of the way the UN has functioned.

North Korea has just seen a transition in power with Kim Jong-un assuming power after the demise of his father. Although North Korea is ostensibly a Socialist state with Communism as its guiding ideology, it has for all practical purposes become an autocratic state with an established dynasty. Kim Jong-un is the third in a line of succession going back to his grandfather, the legendary Kim Il-sung. The new leader has still to establish his leadership qualities and is still in the process of consolidating his power. There are indications of a reshuffle of the top echelons of the party and government leadership, with Kim Jong-un trying to place his loyalists in positions of power. The appointment of Pak Pong-ju as the new PM of North Korea has been welcomed for he is known as an economic reformer and as a pragmatist. By taking a belligerent stand against alleged US and South Korean provocations, Kim hopes to establish his credentials as a "tough" leader who can stand up to the US. This way he hopes to gain the respect of the Party and the Armed Forces. In South Korea too, a dynastic succession of sorts has taken place with the new President, Park, being the daughter of the dictator who ruled South Korea in the 1980s and who was eventually assassinated by his own security chief whilst still in office.

With tight media management the western powers would have most believe that it is the belligerent "north" that threatens the peaceful "south" and that provocations usually emanate from the north. However if the facts are looked at the comparisons between the two halves of the divided peninsula would give quite a different picture. The south is twice as heavily populated as the north (48m to 24m). Its GDP per capita is even more lop-sided (US$ 32,400 to US$ 1,800). As far as military spending is concerned, South Korea spends on an annual basis US$ 26.1 billion as opposed to North Korean annual budget of US$ 8 billion. The equipment, military systems of the south are far superior, equipped as the armed forces of the south are with the latest in US military hardware. There are also elements of two US frontline divisions stationed in South Korea. It would be hard to believe that the US forces are not supported by weapons of mass destruction.

For the US it is not easy to deal with an unpredictable opponent such as the North Koreans. The US does not have the facility of having direct talks with the North Koreans, although it has tried to remedy the situation by sending a series of "special representatives." The Swiss have offered their "good offices" with the Swiss Foreign Ministry stating that "Switzerland is willing to contribute to a de-escalation on the Korean peninsula and is always willing to help find a solution, if this is the wish of the parties, such as hosting meetings between them." No one has as yet taken up the Swiss offer.

The US believes that North Korea violated the 2005 "aid for denuclearisation" deal by not carrying out its obligations negotiated under this deal. The US also believes that the North Koreans violated this agreement by carrying out a nuclear test in 2006. But what has alarmed Washington is the fact that the North Koreans are pursuing a uranium enrichment programme that would give it a second path to a nuclear weapon in addition to its plutonium-based programme. The US is not averse to reopening the six-party talks, but needs assurances regarding the intentions of the North Koreans towards its future nuclear programmes. The US also feels that perhaps the only option left, if progress is to be made, is for the Chinese to put even greater pressure on the North Koreans to "behave." This is the reason why Secretary of State John Kerry hastily visited Beijing in order to seek such assurances.

There is no doubt that the key to finding a solution to the present stalemate lies with Beijing. China is aware of this. China is also aware that the North Koreans do not have many friends left and that particularly after the collapse of the Soviet Union they have no one else to turn to in case the US begins to put unacceptable pressure. Nearly 70 per cent of all North Korean trade is with China and the north is heavily dependent on food, consumer goods, military supplies and financial aid from China. Thus the support of China is crucial for the North Korean regime to survive. On the other hand, the North Koreans also know that no matter how ill-timed their behaviour or how belligerent their policies towards the US and South Korea, at the end of the day China will have no option but to come to their rescue.

For the Chinese, North Korean belligerence towards the US and South Korea is both an opportunity as well as an issue that contains the seeds of future problems. China does not want this verbal belligerence to go viral and thus lead to a conflict from which, as in 1950, it would not be possible for it to stand aside and witness the collapse of the North Korean regime. Thus when Secretary of State Kerry arrived in Beijing, the Chinese sensed that an opportunity had arisen from which it could gain in the strategic stakes. The most interesting Chinese "demand" made to Kerry was that the US "lift and ease" the ban on export of hi-tech items to China! China said that "both countries must shoulder an inescapable responsibility for raising tensions"[3] but curiously put the entire onus on the US. The Chinese also echoed the North Korean position and bluntly stated that "withdrawing US troops from South Korea is the fundamental way to resolve the crisis."[4] To rub it in the Chinese said that they had withdrawn all Chinese troops from North Korea in 1958 and the US was withdrawing troops from Afghanistan, so why can it not withdraw troops from South Korea? Interestingly, China maintained that US troops should continue to stay in Japan to "put down militarism"!

There has been a perceptible shift in the position of US policy in the Asia-Pacific region. It is obvious that with Kerry as the new Secretary of State, the policy followed by former Secretary Clinton was bound to change in emphasis. The Chinese press continues to be hostile to Clinton, but with Kerry the emphasis has shifted to one of cooperation. Thus while the pivot to Asia will perhaps remain unchanged the core would have undergone a substantive change with emphasis now on boosting cooperation with China instead of containment. The US needs Chinese assistance and help not only in dealing with North Korea, but as Kerry himself made clear, the US needs China for tackling the problems of Iran's nuclear ambitions, the question of Syria, nuclear proliferation and bilateral trade issues. It is not for nothing that the US has agreed to hold the 5th Sino-US Strategic and Economic dialogue in July 2013 in the US and that the US National Security Advisor, Tom Donilon, is visiting China in May this year. And as the new Chinese PM, Li Keqiang emphasised to Kerry, the US and China had a "shared responsibility." It would seem that the US has now accepted this proposition.

It is possible that like in the past once the US-South Korean joint "military exercises" are over and the north has less of an incentive to sound belligerent, things would quieten down and the Korean peninsula return to its position of armed peace. As in the past after a period of tension the circle is usually completed with the beginning of another round of negotiations. It is possible that the North Korean leadership is trying the same tactics as before.

There is no doubt that the way forward can only materialise if there are sustained negotiations and continued engagement between the parties concerned. This is not happening at the moment as there are sharp differences of opinion. It is here that the UN can perhaps think of playing a role. Under the UN Charter, Article 33 is quite specific on what needs to be done. Article 33 states that "parties to any dispute, the continuance of which is likely to endanger the maintenance of peace and security, shall first of all seek a solution by negotiation, enquiry, mediation, conciliation, arbitration, judicial settlement, resort to regional agencies or arrangements or other peaceful means of their choice." Therefore a way forward is available for the parties concerned on the Korean peninsula, should they wish to utilise it. However so far the principal UN organ concerned with the maintenance of peace and security has been adopting a policy of "punishment and enforcement" and left the negotiations to the six-party talks. So far, the UNSC's attitude towards the Korean issue has been one of disengagement, rather than one of engagement. Although several UN agencies such as UNDP, WFP,

WHO, UNFPA, FAO, UNICEF are present in North Korea, yet their impact has little effect since their efforts have not been divorced from the political resolutions of the UNSC. It is of fundamental importance that the activities of the UN agencies are humanitarian in nature and not designed to further the political objectives of some influential states.

It is most interesting that an important UN agency, the IAEA, is almost absent from the scene. From the beginning the IAEA has seen its role as one of issuing threats in order to undertake inspections to prevent North Korea from misusing its civilian nuclear programme to convert it for military use. IAEA's role of providing technical assistance for civilian nuclear activities, has in the case of North Korea, been totally missing. On February 25, 2003 the IAEA threatened the North Korean government that in case it did not allow access and inspections of its nuclear facilities, it would refer the case to the UNSC for "action." The result was that North Korea withdrew from the NPT. IAEA's role should have been one of negotiation and engagement and not one of crime and punishment. While no doubt the role of the North Koreans may not have been above board, yet the approach of international agencies too has been fairly one-sided.

There exists an agreement between the US and South Korea that it would not develop a fuel cycle that would lead to enrichment and further ahead to the capability to develop nuclear weapons. This agreement runs out in 2013 and both countries are presently engaged in negotiations on its outcome. The South Koreans have agreed not to undertake any further initiatives in the enrichment process while the talks are in progress.

Nevertheless the remote possibility that the South might also go in for nuclear weapons cannot be ruled out, considering the evolving situation on the Korean peninsula and the general reluctance of the US not to involve itself in conflicts on the East Asian mainland.

Thus as for preventive diplomacy, there is little scope for action as the situation pertains today. As the great powers are deeply involved, their own strategic interests are of importance and would take precedence over other matters. Each side is manoeuvring for greater latitude. Unlike in the past when non-aligned countries such as India had a role to play primarily because the belligerents did not have a channel for communication, no such possibility exists today, for each of the parties is in touch with the other directly. Since the UN Secretary-General is also a former South Korean diplomat he has wisely refrained from offering his "good offices." This is because no matter what position he adopts he would be accused of partisanship. What has to be ensured is that the UN Secretary-General's conduct must be "fair, balanced and objective."

What emerges from the confrontation that is being witnessed today on the Korean peninsula is that any solution is probably dependent upon the condition of the state of play between the two main powers, China and the US. Any solution, if it emerges, will probably be worked out by these two powers. The role of the international community will probably be negligible. There also seems to be very little scope for preventive diplomacy considering that two of the P-5 members are deeply involved.

The following are the UN Security Council Resolutions against North Korea, previous to Resolution 2094 issued on March 13, 2013.

Resolution 1718 (October 14, 2006)

The Security Council, acting under Chapter VII of the UN Charter, unanimously imposed sanctions on North Korea, in reaction to Pyongyang's nuclear test. After arduous negotiations, this softer version establishes an embargo on military and technological materials, as well as luxury goods, but does not include reference to military intervention as the US proposed initially. Furthermore, the resolution demands the freezing of North Korea's financial assets with the exception of funds necessary to meet basic needs.

Resolution 1695 (July 15, 2006)

The 1695 resolution bans all member states from transactions with North Korea involving material, technology or financial resources transfer connected to DPRK's missiles or weapons of mass destruction programmes. In this resolution, the Security Council explicitly condemns the Democratic People's Republic of Korea's (DPRK) nuclear weapons programme. While calling for a diplomatic solution to the situation, the Council demands that the DPRK suspend all activities related to its ballistic missile programme and in this context re-establish its pre-existing commitments to a moratorium on missile launching. It strongly urges the DPRK to return immediately to six-party talks.

Resolution 1540 (April 28, 2004)

Resolution 1540 affirms that non-proliferation of nuclear, chemical and biological weapons, as well as their means of delivery, constitutes a threat to international peace and security. The Security Council urges all States to take additional effective measures to prevent proliferation, including nuclear, chemical or biological weapons and their means of delivery.

Resolution 825 (May 11, 1993)

The Security Council adopted a resolution calling upon North Korea to reconsider withdrawing from the Treaty on Non-proliferation of Nuclear Weapons. The resolution urges North Korea to honour its non-proliferation obligations under the Treaty.

CASE STUDY—SYRIA

When the first wave of enthusiasm swept the Arab world after the Arab Spring had broken out, it was expected that there would be effects on Syria as well, despite the fact that the regime of Bashar Assad was well-entrenched in power. The first eleven months of the Syrian Spring movement were largely peaceful. Some opposition groups that had long sought to establish a democratic form of government in Syria joined hands with the young exuberant demonstrators who had clearly been inspired by the events that were taking place elsewhere in North Africa. In an attempt to dampen down protests the Assad regime took brutal action in May 2011, when 13-year-old Hamza al-Khatib was tortured in detention and his body was thrown on the streets of Daraa for his parents to pick up his mutilated body. In July 2011 a fireman who shouted slogans against the regime had his vocal chords cut and his body mutilated to death. It was the initiation of such atrocities that set the ball rolling and soon the Syrian regime was faced with an unprecedented uprising. Despite sane advice to the contrary, Bashar Assad never apologised for these brutal murders. Perhaps Assad remembered how his father had dealt with similar uprisings in the past. In 1982 the elder Assad had used unprecedented force to put down demonstrations against his regime without suffering any material consequences. Perhaps he also saw what had happened to Hosni Mubarak of Egypt and Ben Ali of Tunisia and he was afraid that a similar fate awaited him.

As the street protests escalated so did the repression. The regime in an effort to silence the opposition arrested the leading members of the secular opposition. This indicated that the regime was not willing for a compromise. At the same time the opposition also indicated that nothing less than the removal of Assad would satisfy them and they too were unwilling for any compromise solution. Thus it was clear that this would be a fight to the finish, with neither side moving an inch from their stated positions.

In order to try and see if there was any space for a compromise solution the UN Secretary-General took the initiative to send two successive envoys to Syria. The first was the former Secretary-General Kofi Annan, and the second was the well-known Algerian diplomat Lakhdar Brahimi.

Kofi Annan was appointed joint UN-Arab League envoy on February 23, 2012 and on March 16, 2012 Kofi Annan presented his 6-point peace plan. The Kofi Annan peace plan contained the following six elements:

- Commit to work with the Envoy in an inclusive Syrian-led political process to address the legitimate aspirations and concerns of the Syrian people, and, to this end, commit to appoint an empowered interlocutor when invited to do so by the Envoy.
- Commit to stop the fighting and achieve urgently an effective United Nations supervised cessation of armed violence in all its forms by all parties to protect civilians and stabilise the country.

  To this end, the Syrian government should immediately cease troop movements towards, and end the use of heavy weapons in, population centres, and begin pullback of military concentrations in and around population centres.

As these actions are being taken on the ground, the Syrian government should work with the Envoy to bring about a sustained cessation of armed violence in all its forms by all parties with an effective United Nations supervision mechanism.

Similar commitments would be sought by the Envoy from the opposition and all relevant elements to stop the fighting and work with him to bring about a sustained cessation of armed violence in all its forms by all parties with an effective United Nations supervision mechanism;

- Ensure timely provision of humanitarian assistance to all areas affected by the fighting, and to this end, as immediate steps, to accept and implement a daily two hour humanitarian pause and to coordinate exact time and modalities of the daily pause through an efficient mechanism, including at local level;
- Intensify the pace and scale of release of arbitrarily detained persons, including especially vulnerable categories of persons, and persons involved in peaceful political activities, provide without delay through appropriate channels a list of all places in which such persons are being detained, immediately begin organising access to such locations and through appropriate channels respond promptly to all written requests for information, access or release regarding such persons;
- Ensure freedom of movement throughout the country for journalists and a non-discriminatory visa policy for them.

- Respect freedom of association and the right to demonstrate peacefully as legally guaranteed.[1]

On March 24, Kofi Annan flew to Moscow to urge the Russian authorities to back fully his peace plan. Following his visit to Moscow, Annan also announced that the Syrian government of Bashar Assad had accepted the peace plan. Annan then met members of the UN Security Council on April 4, 2012 and told them that Assad had assured him that all Syrian troops would leave urban areas by April 12, 2012 and that if this fructifies then the ground would have been laid for positioning 200-300 hundred UN "observers" to be stationed in Syria to observe the ceasefire. However the effort was only half-hearted by both the warring parties and therefore the Syrian government announced that "all relevant elements" would have to give in writing that they would stop giving arms to the rebels before the Syrian army could withdraw from the urban areas. By May 1, 2012 it was clear that neither side was observing the ceasefire proposals seriously. Herve Ladous, the UN Under-Secretary-General for peacekeeping operations announced that "both sides violated the April 12, 2012 ceasefire agreement." Following further bloodshed the Free Syrian army announced that it was launching a general offensive aimed at toppling the Assad regime. In retaliation the Assad government announced that it was reviving operations against the rebels. By now it was clear that neither side was interested in the UN-sponsored initiative. On August 2, 2012 Kofi Annan resigned, stating that the "intransigence of the Assad government and the rebels, as well as the stalemate in the UN Security Council, prevented a peaceful resolution" of the Syrian issue. With this ended the first substantive intervention of the UN on this issue.

When Lakhdar Brahimi took over as the UN envoy after the resignation of Kofi Annan, it was clear that he too would have to develop some kind of a peace plan or at the very least some principles that both sides could accept. Over the next 8 months Brahimi developed five basic parameters that both sides should accept if a political solution was to be found. It was obvious that after nearly two years of intense warfare neither side was any nearer victory. Therefore a military solution was not the answer. In the midst of the fighting the Syrian opposition leader Moaz al-Khatib took the initiative and suggested to the Assad government that as a first step they release all political prisoners, including all women prisoners, as a humanitarian gesture and that the opposition would in return open talks with the government. Even before Assad could give his response, al-Khatib's colleagues shot down the proposal. Thus the room for manoeuvre that had ostensibly opened seemed to close again. In a further hardening of position the Arab League announced that the opposition coalition would in future represent Syria in their meetings. This is not to suggest that there is any semblance of unity amongst the opposition groups. The west for example has its own favourite, Ghassan Hitto who is at loggerheads with al-Khatib.

Brahimi's plan contained the following elements. Firstly, all arms flows to the combatants must stop. However this is not likely to happen unless there is a peace plan or a political process in operation. Secondly, the opposition groups must be more united, with various factions willing to accede to a common credible leadership. In other words the tussles between Hitto and al-Khatib must end as these are often magnified by their respective geopolitical allies. Groups such as the al-Nusra and other Al Qaeda sympathisers, well-known for terrorist activities and identified by the US as such, would have to be eliminated. Thirdly, the opposition groups must give up their dreams of western intervention for neither is it desirable nor feasible. It is doubtful if it can be provoked. The recent entente between Turkey and Israel is not a prelude to an assault. Fourthly, the Assad regime must also give up it dreams of a military victory. In this context the Assad regime must not believe that the existence of the Nusra terror groups along with Al Qaeda affiliates would in any way change the geopolitical realities. The western powers will certainly not ally themselves with the Assad regime in order to defeat these elements.

Even with the Brahimi initiative it is obvious that no solution would be forthcoming so long as the international community remains divided and the fighting in Syria is seen as a sectarian conflict. Nevertheless the Brahimi plan also suffers from some serious shortcomings. These are principally based on the fact that it does not take into account on what happens to the Presidency and to the Security Services in any future dispensation. These are vital questions, for governance in Syria is based on these two very important offices. To leave them for the future would mean that the present plan is rather toothless.

Secondly Brahimi seems to suggest that this is a power struggle and that both sides would be satisfied politically if they are made to share the spoils of office. However the opposition so far has been projecting that it is not so much a struggle for power as for the way they (the Syrians) are governed. They wish for a new political system and an orderly and a gradual process towards democracy. They are not for a splitting of assets. While this might be shear propaganda, nevertheless some semblance of a new order would have to be instituted as otherwise the raison d'être of the opposition groups would be lost. They would be seen as nothing more than a motley crowd jostling for power.

Thirdly Brahimi's own future is in doubt with the Arab League recognising the Syrian Opposition groups and seating them on the Syrian chair within the Arab League Councils. How is his impartiality to be insured when he represents both the UN as well as the Arab League? It seems that the Sunni Arabs have already decided that they have no further use of the services of Brahimi. There are already indications that Brahimi is expected to resign shortly.

The hard fact remains that the Syrian struggle has evolved from a struggle for the restoration of democratic rights into a power struggle in which not only are local actors involved but that it has become a sectarian fight with each side claiming significant external support. A proxy battle of the great powers also seemed in the offing.

The Security Council and later the General Assembly votes on Syria demonstrated vividly that the issue is no longer a question of removing odious dictators deeply entrenched in power by ushering in democracy on the basis of people's power, but that Syria is now spiralling towards a vicious sectarian strife. The battle for a regime change in Syria has also assumed the contours of great power contention. At stake are the immense riches in the energy sector that this region holds. Also on the table are the western attempts to contain, roll back and eliminate Iran's nuclear programme. And for once the Arab-Israeli dispute is on the back burner. Israel is uncharacteristically very quiet, perhaps fearing that Assad's replacement might even be a worse option. At the very least the Assad regime kept the Israeli-Syrian border along the Golan Heights quiet.

The Shiite-Sunni sectarian schism and the struggle for dominance dates far back into history. It occurred soon after the founding of Islam. By bringing the Syrian question to the UN Security Council, on the basis of proposals formulated by the Arab League led principally by the Sunni Arab powers Saudi Arabia and Qatar, the western powers ran the risk of inflaming sectarian opinion. Shiites have seen this as a Sunni-led attempt to oust an Alawite-Shiite-led government. For the western powers to remove a Shiite-led government was a splendid opportunity to strike at the soul of Shiite Iran, one of Syria's foremost supporters. The Syrian Alawite rulers are tough, tenacious and not easily ruffled.

The western failure at the UN Security Council only emboldened the Syrians now assured of Russian and Chinese support. The Assad government has seized this opportunity and have successfully converted what was essentially a movement for the restoration of democracy, into a Sunni-Shiite power struggle. Evidence of this is becoming increasingly apparent in that areas that are dominated by Shiites and other minority groups in Syria are largely peaceful and pro-Assad. There is the fear that fellow Shiite groups such as the Hezbollah and the politically affiliated Hamas would join in the battle and prevent the overthrow of Assad of Syria. And if further proof was needed the Shiite-led government of Iraq, although originally sponsored by the US, has refused to join the anti-Assad bandwagon and on the contrary is actively helping him to survive. Large-scale sectarian strife has broken out in the northern parts of

Iraq where Sunnis battle for political advancement against their Shiite-led government based in Baghdad.

It is indeed a geographical oddity that most of the oil-bearing areas in the Middle East are in areas dominated by the Shiites. Southern Iraq, North-East Saudi Arabia, Bahrain and of course Iran are Shiite areas that come to mind. With the Gulf region holding 27 per cent of the world's oil and 57 per cent of its proven oil reserves along with 45 per cent of the world's natural gas reserves, makes this a very strategic and an immensely important area. And as a former US Vice-President Dick Cheney was to remark, "this is where the prize is"!

By bringing the issue of regime change in Syria to the fore and by going to the UN Security Council, the western powers have tactically made a strategic error. They invited a combined Russian and Chinese veto that has had the effect of cementing their mutual understanding. The greater folly was to push for a plan to "democratise" Syria, based on recommendations made by the Sunni Arab states of Saudi Arabia and Qatar. Saudi Arabia ruled by the Saudi family is as autocratic as any other Arab dictatorship and is hardly a thriving democracy. The sole Qatari contribution to democracy is the hosting of the media giant "Al Jazeera." The western decision has thus resulted only in inflaming opinion along the sectarian divide. The question of Iran's nuclear ambitions and its alleged desire for nuclear weapons has almost entirely been pushed into the background. Iran would of course be delighted if the Syrian issue would continue to hog the limelight and turn into a bitter sectarian fight between Shiites and Sunnis. Great power meddling would only fuel this further.

It is said that Iran is actively pursuing a course of action designed to bolster the Assad regime in Syria. It is been alleged that Iranian commandoes are present in Syria; as are Hezbollah fighters. Therefore the role of Iran in any Syrian settlement assumes importance.

The Shiite rulers of Iran are no pushovers. They are well versed in statecraft and, given the Shiite penchant for sacrifice and martyrdom, are very formidable opponents. The more stringent the sanctions are the more intransigent the Iranians will become. Unlike Saddam Hussein of Iraq who unwittingly walked into a situation by attacking Kuwait and from which he could not retreat, the Iranians are hardly likely to oblige the western powers by blockading the Strait of Hormuz. The Ayatollahs of Iran are far superior in tactics than Saddam ever was and are deeply conscious of the fact that to blockade the Strait of Hormuz would not only put them in the wrong as far as world public opinion is concerned, but would inevitably invite a devastating western military response. Despite incessant bluster emanating from Tehran, the Iranians know that they are no match against combined western military might. In such a scenario while both Russia and China might veto UN resolutions they are hardly likely to risk a military confrontation on behalf of Iran with the western powers.

Iran is an oil and a gas exporting giant that holds 11.1 per cent of the world's proven oil reserves and about 970 b/cm of gas reserves. About 43 per cent of Iranian government expenditures are met from its oil revenues. It would therefore be natural to conclude that if Iranian oil exports could be curtailed, its government would come under severe pressure and would be freed to compromise its nuclear weapons programme. For promoting economic sanctions against Iran, the western powers have been assuring their interlocutors that any shortfall in the crude oil that they imported from Iran would be made up by requesting the Saudis and other Gulf Arab states to make up the necessary shortfall. While this is theoretically possible, this is also the weakest link in the western game plan. North-East Saudi Arabia is the area where most of Saudi oil reserves are situated, it is here that the Saudi oil giant ARAMCO is located and this is also at present the main oil producing area. It is also a Shiite dominated area. There were reports last year of serious sectarian strife in that area which were put down with a heavy hand by the Saudis. The Bahraini movement for democracy which was heavily influenced by local Shiites was put down ruthlessly with the help of Saudi troops specially brought in for that purpose. It was alleged that the agitators had close links with their sectarian co-religionists in Iran. It would therefore be naive to expect that sectarian trouble could not be once again fostered with the help of Iranian sympathy. Should that happen on a sufficiently large scale and for a fairly prolonged period oil prices would inevitably skyrocket northwards. The Saudis would thus be unable to fill the gap created by the Iranian embargo.

On the other hand prolonged strife in the Middle East is something that Russia can quite easily live with. It only adds to its importance as a major strategic player. Russia is today the world's largest producer of oil at about 10 mb/d [million barrels/day] that is slightly more than Saudi Arabia. With its vast network of pipelines it has the ability to switch its oil supply either to the west or eastwards to China, Japan and South Korea. Thus for every dollar increase in the price of oil, Russia stands to gain about seven million dollars per day!

Apart from Israel, a reluctant US and some European countries there is not much popular support for military action against Iran on the nuclear issue. The question of taking armed action is also not receiving enough traction in the United States; where a large majority are not in favour of further US military involvement in the Middle East. The use of the oil embargo weapon to force the issue is also a double-edged one. Apart from EU countries that import 27 per cent of their requirements from Iran, Asian countries such as China, India, Japan and South Korea are also major importers. Therefore any disturbance has major economic implications for most countries, including India. The stability of the world economy would be at stake. Most EU countries would become inordinately dependent on Russian supplies and goodwill. Some EU countries, particularly those in southern Europe with very fragile economies, would probably not survive the economic shock.

Thus while events in Syria unfold, the issues thus generated should not be looked at in a one-dimensional way as merely a fight for the removal of odious dictators. Now that the great powers have taken sides, there are larger and far more dangerous consequences. Awareness of them would go a long way in finding equitable solutions. No solution to the Syrian imbroglio is possible, unless there is great power unity. If the latter becomes possible, a political solution would also emerge. The Syrian case once again demonstrates that international action is quite ineffective, unless it is accompanied by a unity of purpose forged by the great powers.

CHAPTER FIVE

CONCLUSION

The fundamental point that emerges is that there is no one single definition of preventive diplomacy that would satisfy all. The question that then arises is: how is preventive diplomacy any different from normal diplomacy? One explanation offered was that preventive diplomacy was different since the time frames were dissimilar; for preventive diplomacy operates in the short or medium term and in an environment where the intensity of conflict is still moderate.[1] Others felt that preventive diplomacy must be informal, low key, non-binding, non-judgmental, non-coercive and confidential.[2]

Be that as it may, the term preventive diplomacy was first used publicly by the then UN Secretary-General Dag Hammarskjold. His concept was that preventive diplomacy's main function was to prevent a conflict situation from arising between the then two superpowers, the US and Soviet Russia. It was only later that a more comprehensive definition emerged that enlarged the scope and meaning of preventive diplomacy. An attempt was also made for a more holistic and a broader conception of the definition of preventive diplomacy, which underlined that peacekeeping and peace-building were inseparable partners in the quest for a sustainable peace. This approach also emphasised an integrated concept that would be designed to achieve rapid responses based on consent and impartiality of the parties concerned; but with the proviso that ultimately the potential for enforcement could not be ruled out. Nevertheless, it is imperative to go by a definition that perhaps summarises the basics. In a very broad sense the former Secretary-General Boutros-Ghali's definition is perhaps the closest to conceptualising the general view. In his report to the UN Security Council in 1992 entitled "An Agenda for Peace: Preventive Diplomacy, Peace-Making and Peace-Keeping" Boutros Ghali defined preventive diplomacy as follows:

> Action to prevent disputes from arising between parties, to prevent existing disputes from escalating into conflict and to limit the spread of the latter when they occur.

As can be seen Boutros-Ghali's identified three crucial tasks for preventive diplomacy. Firstly, its primary task is to prevent conflict from arising in any part of the world by undertaking preventive steps. Its second task was to prevent existing or ongoing dispute situations from *escalating* (emphasis added) into open conflict and hostilities; and thirdly if the disputes have already broken out into open hostilities, to prevent such a conflict situation from spreading elsewhere. These three are formidable tasks for any person as an individual or for an institution, whether it is international or regional in character, to perform satisfactorily. At present there are no fixed or standard guidelines to follow, nor has any successful attempt been made to institutionalise them. There are no codes that have been worked out and what is available is, at best, the experience gained by international bodies such as the UN. Even this experience gained by the UN in its many initiatives over the years has not been codified or accepted by all stake-holders as useful guidelines. In other words no guidelines or codes acceptable to all the stakeholders are on the table.

Let us consider the first task that has been set for preventive diplomacy which is to prevent conflicts from ever arising. To successfully undertake this task, as a first step, it would be a must to identify potential "hot spots" from where there is a likelihood of conflict situations arising. To do so would require personnel that are exceptionally talented and experienced in political issues. They should be able to draw attention immediately to potential "hot spots." Secondly, unlike in the past where a dearth of information was the norm, there is today to the contrary a mass of information that is available. This is partly due to the media revolution, technological advances and instant communications. With the extensive data that is now available what is therefore required are trained political operatives who can sift, diagnose and prioritise the information as it arrives. It goes without saying that such personnel must be politically neutral, experienced in the ways of international diplomacy and above all impartial. They must not be seen as advocating a particular political ideology or a particular economic stance for otherwise trust in their judgement would be easily impaired. On the other hand, if every piece of information that is available is required to be acted upon, then a situation may arise where the decision-makers are inundated with a mass of information which might then degenerate to no action at all. In many cases the information may be dated and not of much value. It is therefore essential that a choice has to be made, priorities established and only the most important cases are then selected for action.

In this respect both the Office of the United Nations High Commissioner for Human Rights (OHCHR) and the Office of the Special Adviser for the Prevention of Genocide and Mass Atrocities are playing a key role in filtering information and drawing attention to perceived dangerous indicators such as patterns of human rights violations or hate speech, which might otherwise escape detection. Similarly, closer cooperation between the United Nations and regional organisations such as the African Union and ECOWAS, both of which operate early warning systems, have ensured more and better data. It is not anybody's case that action must be taken on each and every case.

The second task is both fairly easy to perform as also quite difficult. The question is, why is there this obvious dichotomy in approach? If a conflict has already broken out and the attempt is to contain and to prevent it from spreading, the crucial point that emerges is: what are the chances of the international community having a uniform view on the proposed action? The question really is not about suppressing, eliminating or containing a conflict situation or violence that has arisen by using superior force, but it is a question of utilising a range of formal and informal activities to limit and reduce the level of violence and to undertake an exercise to understand the key issues involved. The Peace Research Institute of Oslo has documented all the conflicts since 1945 that have had more than 25 fatalities. The figure that the Oslo Institute has arrived is 1,776 such conflicts. The interesting statistics are that of the 1,776 such conflicts listed by the Oslo Institute, about 1,540 or 86.7 per cent are listed as "internal" conflicts. Most such internal conflicts stem from poverty, deepening social inequalities, corrupt governance and a proliferation of political factions based on religious or ethnic lines. These figures clearly indicate that these are social and economic issues that need to be addressed. Clearly force would have very little role to play.

As the Oslo Institute has shown most of the post Second World War conflicts have been "internal" in nature and therefore even international financial institutions have realised that they too have a constructive responsibility in this regard. The World Bank has set up a post-conflict reconstruction unit as a part of its holistic approach to understanding the issues of peace and conflict resolution. In the Bank's view there is a positive link between conflict and developmental issues. To prove its contention the Bank cites the fact that of the 20 poorest countries in the world, at least 15 have been in a state of conflict in the last twenty years. The danger that this represents is that in most cases such a conflict has the tendency to spill over into neighbouring countries, leading to social and economic disintegration. The World Bank feels that its mission is to "facilitate" a transition to sustainable peace after hostilities have ceased. The Bank supports development activities in order to help countries facing conflict situations to reconstruct, thus creating situations for a functioning peace-time society. Although many conflicts have as their base ethnic and religious animosities, yet the underlying factors beneath these manifestations are more complex and impinge upon economic, social and political relationships. International financial institutions strongly feel that creating conditions for a functioning peace-time society is a must for ensuring long-term peace and security. The crucial question that thus emerges is: can there be unanimity within the international community on how to address such issues, be they political, economic or social? Does a will exist within the international community for such deliberate action?

On a more hopeful note if by some chance a substantial agreement emerges from within the international community on the proposed action, then it becomes fairly easy to implement. Further if there is unanimity within the P-5, then it becomes even much easier. In such a scenario, no two states that are in conflict can flout the views of the international community, particularly of the P-5, with ease or with impunity. Similarly in intra-state conflict situations, if there is unanimity within the international community, then whatever methods that are devised to attend to the situation will have much greater chances of success. If states wish to flout international opinion then the consequences for them, both political and economic, would be beyond their capacity to bear. The key point therefore is that there must be unanimity within the international community on the proposed action.

The problem that arises is when there is no unanimity within the international community or within the P-5 powers, on the proposed action to be taken. All great powers have foreign policy aspirations based upon their assessment of their net power projections. Although some analysts perceive the United States as a declining power, yet by any standards, it is still the world's sole superpower, both politically, militarily and economically, and likely to remain so for the immediate future. Thus the US has the capability of projecting this power in most parts of the world. It also means that the US, in order to maintain this superiority, has certain political and economic imperatives. For example, the US is extremely sensitive to any turbulence in the Middle

East because the bulk of its energy imports come from that region. That was the reason why it acted with such alacrity, as our case study shows, when Saddam Hussein of Iraq decided in 1990 to invade and occupy Kuwait. Conversely, when Turkey invaded and occupied the northern half of

Cyprus, there was no call for internationally sponsored action to oust Turkey from northern Cyprus, even though Cyprus is a sovereign, independent nation. It can be said that no key interest of any great power was involved in the Turkish action and therefore Turkey did not suffer any major consequences of its military action against the sovereign independent republic of Cyprus. Cynics allege that there was no action because northern Cyprus has no great economic resources to exploit! Similarly, when Israel undertakes any military action in its neighbourhood, even if it is considered to be an infringement of international law by the international community, it gets away with it because of US political protection, since Israel is a factor in domestic US politics. Between 1996 and 2003, the US exercised its right of veto nine times and interestingly out of the nine, eight were Israel related vetoes! In present times it is the US that is the main user of Veto in the United Nations Security Council.

Similarly Russia, when its strategic interests were threatened in the Caucasus, had no compunction in invading and slicing off the two provinces of the independent state of Georgia (South Ossetia and Abkhazia) to settle the issue. Much as the western countries tried, and the EU temporarily even threatened sanctions, but nothing came out of the situation, despite western fulminations, for as a great power Russia could not be challenged.

Apart from obtaining unanimity from within the international community there are still other options available, although they may not be as successful in the absence of great power support. These measures, apart from the "good offices" of the UN Secretary-General or his nominee, range from negotiation, mediation, conciliation, arbitration and judicial settlement. Successive UN Secretaries-General have tried to use their "good offices" by nominating important personalities to try and see if it was possible to diffuse the situation by preventing the spread of violence. In the case studies undertaken of the conflict situations in Libya, Syria, Iraq, Iran and North Korea the impact of UN Secretary-General sponsored "good offices" was assessed.

As it would be tedious to mention all cases, let us examine the case of Libya where the present UN Secretary-General nominated the former Foreign Minister of Jordan, Abdel-Elah al-Khatib to represent him in the negotiations between the two opposing parties. The choice of al-Khatib was in many ways unfortunate. He came from a state (Jordan) that was actively involved, in conjunction with its western partners, in the overthrow of the Gaddafi regime. Secondly, being an Arab he had been an active participant in domestic Arab politics and therefore could hardly be expected to be neutral in his dealing with the Libyan parties. Al-Khatib described his mission as follows:

"We are trying to encourage both parties to respond to our ideas about certain ways to handle the situation—to agree to a ceasefire linked to a political transitional process. People are conducting these talks with the UN, so we are going back and forth between them, listening to their views and encouraging them to engage on a more sustainable basis with us. The issues to be addressed are complex. What would a political transition look like? What interim political structures could be put in place, and who will be represented in them? How long would the transition last? What are the necessary reforms to ensure a democratic future for the Libyan people? My most recent discussions have focused on getting both sides to define their views on these points as a basis for negotiations to move forward.

"I think the UN is bound with what is in the Security Council resolutions, especially resolution 1973, which calls for an immediate, comprehensive ceasefire for addressing the humanitarian needs and providing humanitarian protection for the Libyan people and also for fulfilling the legitimate demands of the Libyan people—this is the mandate in the Security Council resolution. And this is where the United Nations stands on this. Ultimately, it will be up to the Libyan people to decide their future, the way in which they wish to be governed and the country to be ruled. Having said this, clearly there can be no return to the status quo that existed before the crisis."

In other words Gaddafi had to go. But what if the Libyan people wanted a return to the status quo? As per al Khatib's own words, he hardly sounded impartial! Clearly, as seen from his own words, the UN Special Envoy for Libya was acting more in line with the thinking of the western powers who were determined on a regime change.

Similar was the fate of the two UN Secretary-General's Special Envoys to Syria, Kofi Annan and Lakhdar Brahimi. Both did not succeed as the agendas of the great powers were different. Whilst Russia and China supported the Assad regime, the western powers were keen on its ouster. In fact all that the latter wished to see was a regime change.

Since the military push by the rebels for a regime change did not succeed, the two UN Envoys were left with a very unenviable task! One has resigned and the other, according to last reports, is on the verge of doing so.

Take the Iran-Iraq War. Saddam Hussein attacked Iran on September 22, 1980 and for four days there was no meeting of the UN Security Council. Between September 26, 1980 and October 24, 1980, the UN Security Council met six times. It was only on the second meeting on September 28, 1980 that it passed UN Security Council Resolution 479 that called for an end to the fighting. Significantly, Resolution 479 did not condemn or even mention Iraqi aggression, nor did it call for Iraqi forces to return to internationally recognised borders. To refresh the politics of the time; Saddam Hussein was the "friend" of the western powers. Iran rightly rejected this resolution as being completely one-sided, as it so was. To make amends somewhat, the UN Secretary-General Kurt Waldheim at first offered his "good offices" and when that did not find any takers he appointed Olaf Palme as his special representative in November 1980. Palme mission too was a failure. The failure was entirely due to the fact that the Iranians did not trust Kurt Waldheim for his alleged "closeness" to the Shah of Iran and the fact that his dealings in the hostage crisis were seen by the Iranians as being partisan. Incidentally Iraq was not branded as an aggressor till 1991, by which time Saddam Hussein had fallen foul of the western powers.

As regards North Korea the UN seems to have washed its hands off completely and left it to the six nation talks to resolve the issues.

Let us now take the third task assigned to preventive diplcmacy, namely to prevent the spread of violence in a conflict situation and if possible to try and end the fighting as quickly as possible. The nature of conflict that we witness at present has changed significantly starting from the end of the cold war period. It is no longer an interstate conflict, where the mechanisms developed since the end of the Second World War apply. Most post-Cold War conflicts are now intra-state or within the territorial boundaries of a state. Such conflicts tend to be civil, regional, internal and intra-communal conflicts in nature. Peace is now not considered to be the absence of war, but a positive progression towards conflict resolution, rebuilding of torn societies and their eventual reconciliation. Therefore, the nature of the response of the international community has also undergone a change, to some extent at least. Relatively newer approaches that include such concepts as facilitation and truth and reconciliation have recently been developed for the peaceful resolution of disputes. Whilst the UN system has by perforce to cater to the inviolability of state sovereignty and the non-interference in a state's internal affairs, there is a growing movement that supports the concept of "people sovereignty" and not "state sovereignty." This is because in a world where there is increasing violence the majority of casualties are not members of the armed forces, but civilians. It is a situation where failed states are incapable of defending their populations from the ravages of internal conflict and where terrorism has found a safe haven. It is a situation where identity conflicts predominate and abject poverty is a common phenomenon. Thus situations such as these would not be conducive for a peaceful solution if the tools devised to uphold state sovereignty and state security are used as the primary methods for a solution. In such situations, it may become necessary for "humanitarian" interventions by the international community.

The arrival of terrorism and non-state actors has complicated immensely the search for solutions. Terrorism defies prevalent laws and values and in an age of illicit financing is able to transcend state boundaries and find refuge primarily in failed states. Forces of globalisation have opened state boundaries and linked societies globally, with unlimited access to information technology. Thus as technology has gone global so has terrorism. Therefore the need is to devise new and more appropriate methods to deal with such conflict situations.

It must be said at the outset that preventive diplomacy is also an evolving concept. Neither in its concepts nor in its methods is it static. Whilst the methods adopted soon after the conclusion of the Second World War had relevance then, these concepts too have developed over time with newer challenges as the world has become ever closer together with the ongoing information and communication technology revolution. Nevertheless, there are still some basic requirements that need to be fulfilled before success can be claimed for preventive diplomacy. Just as peace is presently not thought of as simply the absence of war, so too preventive diplomacy is not seen as simply the prevention of conflict. It is now thought to encompass something much more. Preventive diplomacy is now thought of as also a progression towards building a consensus towards reconciliation, a rebuilding of shattered societies and creating situations where it is possible to build an atmosphere where peace can endure. Towards these ends the following are absolute imperatives for successful missions of preventive diplomacy.

The first requirement is resource mobilisation. At a time when most states are facing an economic downturn, it becomes extremely difficult to propose additional outlays for international peacekeeping purposes, particularly when a conflict has yet to take shape and the additional financial outlays are only for anticipated problem areas. Most finance ministries have the natural tendency to postpone such decisions when there are more pressing internal problems that require instant attention. Similar is the stated reaction of politicians, for such ventures do not have a vote catching potential. International disputes, even if they are at an incipient stage, are rarely popular and most states tend to stay away unless their own national interests are involved. It is here that the role played by the media becomes important. We are living in a world today where there is instant communication. Today the media has the ability through the development of technologies, the placement of press representatives and practices to bring the reality and the grim outcome of a conflict into the homes of almost every citizen. The media can play a very important role in conflict prevention, reconstruction and peace building, simply by bringing the issues and its ramifications into the domain of domestic politics. Since domestic politics can be affected it is possible that hitherto dithering politicians can morph into action to try and put a stop to an impending conflict. One of the strongest arguments that can be deployed for preventive diplomacy is that it costs practically very little, even quite modest, if the issue is resolved at the very early incipient stage; for its costs are likely to be that much higher and can even escalate exponentially if intervention takes place much after the conflict has already broken out. This then is a task before the UN system and its staff to put forward these persuasive arguments to convince states that it is much more cost-effective to take action now than later. It can become even more persuasive if examples are cited where early action might have saved considerable expenditure. Since it is no one's case that financial commitment be open-ended, it is important to ensure that preventive diplomatic action is also not open-ended. Before it is contemplated, how to conclude the "action" should also be included in the proposals. It is vital that a time frame be settled also.

Whilst the question of raising sufficient financial resources is crucial, the question of obtaining the necessary manpower to "police" a conflict situation is also very important. The UN has no soldiers of its own and it is therefore dependent on the contributions made by member states. Trained manpower, particularly trained soldiers, are difficult to locate, simply because most states have already deployed their own soldiers for duty and do not have sufficient surplus manpower left for deployment for international duty. If the present UN deployment patterns are to be seen, much of the manpower comes from the South Asian states of India, Pakistan, Bangladesh and Nepal. Even Germany, which still has one of the larger armies in Europe, finds it difficult to spare troops for international duty, but this may be because some of its troops are deployed with NATO in Afghanistan.

The next requirement is flexibility. There is no question that there is ever a case for one solution fitting all requirements. Every issue or a problem has a dynamic and a momentum of its own and therefore it requires a sophisticated understanding of the conflict setting and of its principals. There has to be a nuanced understanding of the history, political and cultural milieu of the issues and of the combatants. It is important to understand the underlying causes of the grievances that led to a conflict-like situation arising. Sometimes grievances may be imaginary or petty, but it is important to understand the context in which they have been raised. They should not be dismissed out of hand as simply petty and therefore not worthy of attention. In the world today, particularly in the context of globalisation, most of the grievances may be economic in nature, or that a group of influential politicians are simply squandering away precious natural resources for personal pelf and advantage. It is not above consideration that some external powers may be fuelling conflict simply to gain advantage over the natural resources that a state holds. Therefore in the international context, whenever a conflict situation arises and it is to be handled by utilising the concept of preventive diplomacy, the personnel involved must be flexible in judgement and approach. Their diagnoses of the situation would be a critical input in the eventual success of the mission. In the context of the UN or some other regional organisation that undertakes preventive diplomacy, these important points relating to a flexible approach must be kept in mind. It goes without saying that the personnel so selected, particularly by the UN system or by regional organisations must be impartial, fair and have a deep understanding of the historical and political context of issues involved in that particular setting. A sympathetic approach would indeed be exceedingly useful.

The next requirement is a receptive political context. In recent times conflict has become intra-state rather than interstate. Between the years 1989 and 1992 the number of intra-state and ethnic conflicts dramatically increased. It is estimated that of the 82 conflicts that took place during this period, about 79 were intra-state. Therefore the essence is in dealing with intra-state issues. Thus if both parties to a dispute that is essentially internal, *agree* (emphasis added) to receive external help for resolving such a dispute, then nothing could be a better platform to launch a preventive diplomacy mission. This however does not obviate the necessity for a complete and exhaustive study that must be undertaken of the issues involved. This exercise should involve a study of the behaviour patterns of the combatants, their values and attitudes. In a situation where the parties to the dispute are fractured with no recognisable leadership, it becomes important to establish whether they are in any position to come to terms and if they are, would they be capable of implementing the same? It is important to determine whether there is a legitimate leadership in position or not. Sometimes in situations where there has been an intra-state conflict, often the elected leadership has been ejected and new leaders emerge whose credentials are based solely on the strength of the force that they command. It is not uncommon for coups and counter coups to take place within a short space of time. Therefore the staying power of a group that claims power must also be assessed.

In the case of failed states the problem becomes even more acute for there is no recognisable leadership available. The leadership has simply disappeared or has been murdered and eliminated. This then leaves the space open for combatants who in the very nature of things are nothing but armed gangs operating, more as armed thugs, than any recognisable political force. It is here that another issue also comes to the fore and that is the question of "boy soldiers" and of gender mass murder and rape of women. All these are the manifestations of a failed state. Therefore, in the context of preventive diplomacy, it would not only be a question of ensuring peace, but taking steps towards reconstruction and rebuilding state institutions so that a peace environment can be ensured. These are major tasks and therefore an assessment is necessary since entering a situation that is open-ended may not be very conducive for success. No external agency, whether it is international or regional, likes open-ended commitments.

Finally, there is the question of enforcement. The former Foreign Minister of Australia, Gareth Evans had put forward the view that three conditions should be met before the use of force could be considered. These were (1) just cause (2) right intention and (3) last resort. By "just cause" it was clarified that intervention should only take place where there had been a large-scale loss of life which led to action that had a genocidal intent and where there had been large-scale ethnic cleansing followed by mass terror and rape as an instrument of policy. There is no doubt that these "conditions," if followed, would take care of the suspicion in the minds of some states and institutions or concerned people, that military intervention was planned for taking sides in the internal struggle for power or that it was being undertaken with ulterior motives. Sometimes suspicion is aroused when the affected area is resource rich and intervention is seen for economic advantage. Other scholars have opined that enforcement should only take place when there is a threat to international peace and security and where there has been a massive violation of human rights.

If a situation arises where intervention is necessary and where the use of force is contemplated and if this has international approval, the decision becomes that much easier to take. Here it is important that "intentions" of those advocating enforcement be completely above board. In this context newly independent states are particularly wary that advantage is being taken of the fragility of their political processes to reintroduce the ex-colonial power into their domestic situations. Therefore they are very reluctant to agree to external intervention. The sanctity of the state is one of the bedrocks of the international system and no matter what the cause, states are as a general rule very reluctant to allow international intervention into their domestic affairs. Therefore it goes without saying that the "cause" must be just, before intervention is contemplated. What the critics allege is that intervention is never universal in its approach. If it is a question of protecting human rights, then why is it protected in some cases and ignored in others? Civil wars, persecutions, widespread torture, forced refugees and tyrannical behavior occur in most parts of the world and yet the response is only limited and in selected areas only. It is a flawed response. Take Tibet, for example. Due to systematic persecution there have been a series of self-immolations there and yet because China is a P-5 power, no one has raised this issue at the international level. Even the UN High Commissioner for Human Rights, ever so voluble and eloquent elsewhere, is knowingly low-key in her statements.

On the other hand, the international community cannot simply sit and watch a whole people being massacred and not intervene in the name of protecting state sovereignty. As the then UN Secretary-General Kofi Annan had remarked:

> If humanitarian intervention is, indeed, an unacceptable assault on sovereignty, how should we respond to a Rwanda, to a Srebrenica—to gross and systematic violations of human rights?

The World Summit in 2005 recognised this important issue and commended humanitarian intervention in its declaration. Both the UN General Assembly and the Security Council have also recognised the efficacy of this method. Nevertheless, when force is contemplated or being actively considered it must be proportional to the requirement. If a simple short and sharp engagement, or even the threat of use of force, can achieve the necessary results, then there is no need to consider a long-term deployment or a deployment of considerable force. Invariably the question is raised as to who will authorise the use of force and who will decide when to terminate such action? If the international community is of one mind, then it is best if the UN Security Council is left to do the decision-making, since it is this body that has been authorised to take action under the UN Charter. Unilateral action or action by a "coalition of the willing" will always be suspect and as being entirely motivated by other considerations.

There is no doubt that the use of force has to be a matter of last resort. There is no question that, unless all other alternatives have been tried and have failed to achieve their objective, only then should the use or the threat of the use of force be contemplated. Sometimes if the impression is reinforced that if preventive diplomacy fails it would lead to military action, this can have a salutary effect. In present times with the information and communication technology (ICT) revolution in place, no part of the world is immune from witnessing the horrors of humanitarian violations that often take place in the far corners of the world. The Information and Communication Technology revolution now transcends geographical boundaries. The media, if it wishes to play a positive role, can be a force for peace and stability and an important player in conflict transformation. By being a vehicle for expressing genuine grievances and emotions and presenting a case for intervention when required, in cases where mass genocide, ethnic cleansing or mass rape have taken place, it can play a very useful role in making military intervention possible and acceptable universally.

Finally, the question must be asked: Is preventive diplomacy capable of delivering results? There is no doubt that the logic of preventive diplomacy is impeccable. As the adage goes "pay now or pay much more later," sums up its inherent usefulness. It is also difficult to measure success or failure in absolute terms, for in either case there are many more ingredients involved. There is also no doubt that the world is still an unequal playing field. The great powers of the day are much more likely to have their way and the ultimate test still remains old-fashioned power play. So while preventive diplomacy is being undertaken, its success may also be due other actions that are taking place simultaneously. Therefore its success may not be entirely of its making.

There is also no doubt that there have been many missed chances. Take for example, the break up of Yugoslavia. It is estimated that about ¼ million people died, 200,000 were wounded and over 1 million displaced. There is no denying the horrors of genocide in Rwanda or the failed state of Somalia. On the other hand, Macedonia did not fall into mass violence and in the Congo tribal and ethnic divisions were contained (the successes as listed by the UN Department of Political Affairs are at Annexure I).

Could it be then that the concept of preventive diplomacy has been oversold as a positive contributor towards maintaining world peace? Not if you were to consider what the UN Secretary-General said. This is what he has said:

Preventive diplomacy today is delivering concrete results, with relatively modest resources, in many regions of the world, helping to save lives and to protect development gains. It is an approach that may not be effective in all situations and will continue to face the uncertainty, risks and evolving challenges which, in a sense, come with the terrain. However, I firmly believe that better preventive diplomacy is not optional; it is necessary.

This, it seems, is a fair conclusion.

ANNEXURE-1

Q: What are some recent cases in which the United Nations used preventive diplomacy to ease tensions?

A: There are a number of cases noted in the report in which concerted preventive action by the United Nations and its partners helped to avert or contain conflict. For example: In Sudan, preventive diplomacy was a major focus of international efforts—led for the United Nations by its peacekeeping mission—to ensure the successful holding of the January 2011 independence referendum for Southern Sudan. The Security Council was actively engaged, including through its statements and visits to the country. The Secretary-General appointed a high-level panel that also encouraged actions and agreements to permit the smooth holding of the referendum.

In Guinea, from 2009 to 2010 the United Nations Office for West Africa (UNOWA) worked energetically to keep on track a political transition from a military coup to the country's first democratic elections since independence.

In Sierra Leone, the United Nations Integrated Peacebuilding Office in Sierra Leone (UNIPSIL) helped prevent the potential escalation of violence following tensions between the governing and opposition parties in 2009.

In Iraq, the United Nations Assistance Mission for Iraq (UNAMI) has facilitated peaceful dialogue over Kirkuk and other disputed internal territories, and assisted in smoothing the path to elections in 2009 and 2010.

In Kenya, following the outbreak of post-electoral violence in 2008, the United Nations quietly provided strong support to the African Union-led mediation efforts that succeeded in stopping the violence and resolving the political-electoral conflict through negotiations.

In Kyrgyzstan, the United Nations Regional Centre for Preventive Diplomacy for Central Asia (UNRCCA) worked closely with key governments and regional organisations such as the OSCE to encourage an end to the 2010 inter-ethnic violence and a return to constitutional order. The office is also encouraging agreements on the peaceful sharing of water resources in the region.

In the Democratic Republic of the Congo (DRC), the timely dispatch of an envoy of the Secretary-General in autumn 2008 helped to quell unrest and ease tensions between Rwanda and the DRC that might have deteriorated into renewed regional war.

NOTES

CHAPTER ONE
WHAT IS THE MEANING OF PREVENTIVE DIPLOMACY?

1. Lund, *Early Warning and Preventive Diplomacy: A Strategy for Preventive Diplomacy*, 1996, pp. 39-44.
2. Evans, 1994, pp. 14-17.
3. Simon S. C. Tay, Obood Talib, ARF, "Preparing for Preventive Diplomacy," *Contemporary South-East Asia*, vol. 19, no. 3, December 1997, 236.
4. Andrew Cordier, Wilder Foote: Public Papers of UN Secretaries-General: Dag Hammarskjold, vol. 5, Columbia University Press cited in Acharaya, "Preventive Diplomacy: Background and Application," pp. 16-17.
5. Ibid., p. 17
6. Annan 2002. J. Ododa Opiyo, *The Challenges of Preventive Diplomacy: The United Nation's post-Cold War Experiences in Africa.*
7. United Nations Security Council 2000. J. Odada Opiyo, ibid.
8. Steven Zyck and Robert Muggah, *Preventive Diplomacy and Conflict Prevention*, p. 69.
9. Michael S. Lund, *Preventing Violent Conflict: A Strategy for Preventive Diplomacy.*
10. Mohammed Bedjaoui, *The Fundamentals of Preventive Diplomacy*, p. 30.
11. Heather Hamilton, *Briefing Book on UN Preventive Diplomacy*, p. 4.
12. C. Gray, *International Law and the Use of Force*, Oxford University Press, 2000.
13. Boutros-Ghali, Supplement to an Agenda for Peace, UN Document A/50/60, January 3, 1995, p. 3.
14. Ibid, p. 8.

15. Heather Hamilton, *Briefing Book on UN Preventive Diplomacy*, p. 17.
16. Quoted by former Australian Foreign Minister Gareth Evans.
17. Quoted by former Australian Foreign Minister Gareth Evans.
18. Zartman, *Preventive Negotiation: Avoiding Conflict*, 2005, p. 20.
19. Gareth Evans.
20. World Bank: 2011, *World Development Report—Conflict, Security and Development*.
21. Gareth Evans.

CHAPTER TWO
SOME BASIC PRINCIPLES OR GUIDELINES FOR PREVENTIVE DIPLOMACY

1. ICJ REP., 1969, p. 3/North Sea Continental Shelf.
2. Speech at University of California, 1955.
3. Preventive Diplomacy: Report of the Secretary-General, S/2011/552 dated August 26, 2011.
4. Report of UN Secretary-General, August 26, 2011.
5. Institute de Droit International, Article 1.
6. Report of UN Secretary-General, August 26, 2011.
7. Report of UN Secretary-General, August 26, 2011.
8. Report of UN Secretary-General, August 26, 2011.
9. Resolution 65/283.
10. Report of UN Secretary-General, August 26, 2011.

CHAPTER THREE
A STRATEGY FOR IMPLEMENTATION

1. Carnegie Commission Final Report, pp. 37, 69.
2. *Opportunities Missed and Seized*, edited by Bruce Jentleson.
3. Stefan Wolff, CBM: An Overview of Elite Level Options, University of Birmingham.
4. Kalha, *The Ultimate Prize*, Allied, 2008, p. 46.
5. International Policy Analysis, "Global Threats and the Role of UN Sanctions," FES, New York, December 2011.
6. The Graduate Institute, Geneva.

7. Watson Institute for International Studies, Brown University.
8. UN: Principles and Guidelines for Peace Keeping Operations.
9. Gareth Evans, Symposium on Humanitarian Intervention, University of Wisconsin, March 31, 2006.
10. C. A. J. Coady, *The Ethics of Armed Humanitarian Intervention*, US Peace Institute, July 2002.
11. Ibid.

CASE STUDY—IRAN

1. Garver, *China's Assistance to Iran's Nuclear Programme*, Chapter 6, pp. 156-58.
2. Reuters, November 4, 2011.
3. Debka-file/Israel.
4. Scott Harold, Alireza Nader, *China and Iran—Economic, Political and Military Relations.*
5. Reuters, October 10, 2010.
6. Press TV, February 16, 2013.
7. MEES Article, vol. XLV, no. 34; August 2002.
8. Adam Levine, CNN, March 5, 2013.
9. Shi Yinhong, East Asia Forum, May 17, 2011.

CASE STUDY—IRAQ

1. Kalha, *The Ultimate Prize*, p. 201.
2. King, *UN and the Iran-Iraq War 1980-88*, pp. 14-16.
3. Fisk, *The Great War for Civilisation*, p. 257.
4. NYT, August 18, 2002.
5. Woodward, "CIA Aiding Iraq in the Gulf War," *Washington Post*, December 15, 1986. See also Woodward, "Veil: The Secret Wars of the CIA 1981-87" (Simon & Schuster), p. 480.
6. *New Yorker Magazine*, "Bush's Secret Mission," November 2, 1992.
7. *Washington Post*, December 15, 1986.
8. Kalha, *The Ultimate Prize*, p. 185.
9. Robert Fisk, *The Great War for Civilization*, p. 73.
10. Telegram from Secretary Baker for DPM Tariq Aziz, October 12, 1989, page 3 of 4, State 338562C 12/25 009007 NOD 191.

11. Woodward, *The Commanders*, pp. 203-4.
12. Defence Intelligence Agency, Gulf War Chronologies.
13. Ibid.
14. Kalha, *The Ultimate Prize*, pp. 217-18.
15. Murray Wass, *Who lost Kuwait?* pp. 30, 38.
16. NYT, January 24, 1991, p. D22.
17. *Kuwaiti Times*, August 2.
18. *Washington Post*, March 8, 1991, p. A26.
19. NYT, September 23, 1990.
20. Fisk, *The Great War for Civilization*, p. 724.
21. See also Freedman and Karsh, *The Gulf Conflict*, pp. 47-63.
22. See *Foreign Policy Magazine*, January-February 2003.
23. See also Claude Rakisits, *The Gulf Crisis: The Failure of Preventive Diplomacy*, Allen & Unwin, 1994, pp. 58-103.
24. Reference is to a Congressional Research Report [CRS] prepared by Lawrence Cummins. It can be accessed at Kalha, *The Ultimate Prize* (New Delhi: Allied Publishers, 2008), p. 248.

CASE STUDY—LIBYA

1. Colin Moynihan, NYT, February 21, 2011.
2. Provisional Rules of Procedure of the Security Council refers to Article 35 of the Charter referring to "nations that are Members of the UN" or "nations that are not Members of the UN." Nowhere does it provide for defecting officials to request a meeting of the Security Council.
3. Ronda Hauben, "The Role of the UN Security Council in Unleashing an Illegal War against Libya," July 20, 2011.
4. Closed Meeting Security Council, no notes but the occurrence of the meeting is noted as 6486 Meeting (closed). Peace and Security in Africa, February 22, 2011, http://www.un.org/Docs/ journal/En/20110223e.pdf.
5. Lynn Pascoe, Informal comments to the media by B. Lynn Pascoe, Under-Secretary-General for Political Affairs, on the situation in Libya, February 22, 2011, http://www.unmultimedia.org/tv/webcast/2011/02/b-lynn-pascoe-on-the-situation-in-libya.htm.
6. See video of Ambassador Shalgham, February 22, 2011, http://www.

youtube.com/user/NizarAbboud#p/search/0/fKhMUSHwtrA) http://www.unmultimedia.org/tv/webcast/2011/02/b-lynn-pascoe-on-the-situation-in-libya.htm.

7. Press Release, Organisation of the Islamic Conference, OIC General Secretariat Condemns Strongly the Excessive Use of Force against Civilians in the Libyan Jamahiriya [February 22, 2011], available at http://tinyurl.com/62rmq75.
8. African Union Peace and Security Council, Dec. PSC/PR/COMM (CCLXI), 2/February 23, 2011.
9. Mehrdad Payandeh, The UN, Military Intervention and Regime Change in Libya.
10. Ronda Hauben, "The Role of the UN Security Council in Unleashing an Illegal War against Libya," July 20, 2011.
11. UN Doc. S/RES/1970/Feb.26,2011.
12. "Abuse of UN Processes in Security Council Actions against Libya" (RondaHauben.netcolumnist@gmail.com)
13. Ibid.
14. Ibid.
15. Ibid.
16. Ibid.
17. Ibid.
18. Reference from AP Report, March 22, 2011.
19. Letter from Libyan Government to President, Security Council. Document no. S/2011/161.
20. "Abuse of UN Processes in Security Council Actions against Libya" (RondaHauben.netcolumnist@gmail.com)
21. Curtis Doebbler, "Libya: Who Wins?" Al Ahram, April 7-13, 2011, issue no. 1012.
22. According to General Assembly Resolution 396(V) of December 1950, it is for the General Assembly to decide who should represent a State.

CASE STUDY—NORTH KOREA (THE DEMOCRATIC REPUBLIC OF KOREA–DPRK)

1. US Amb To Secretary of State/December 18, 1950, File No.793B.00/12-1850.
2. British Foreign Office Records. File No. 371-84454.
3. Chen Fengjun, *Global Times*, April 17, 2013.
4. GT, ibid.

CASE STUDY—SYRIA

1. UNSC Meeting 6736, March 21, 2012, Presidential Statement. See also Douglas Hamilton, Reuters, April 4, 2012.

CHAPTER FIVE
CONCLUSION

1. Lund, 1996, pp. 39-44.
2. Evans, 1994, pp. 14-17.

AUTHORS PROFILE

Ranjit Singh Kalha, born in Lahore (now Pakistan) on February 25, 1942, did his Masters in 1964 in History from Punjab University, Chandigarh. He was awarded a Gold Medal for standing first in the University.

Mr. Kalha was selected for the Indian Foreign Service in 1965 and subsequently studied at the University of Hong Kong where he attained fluency in the Chinese language.

He has held the important posts of Joint Secretary for Americas and for East Asia dealing with China, Japan, etc. He led the Indian side for the India-China Boundary Sub-Group Negotiations for the period 1985-88.

Mr. Kalha served as India's Ambassador to Indonesia (1988-92) and Iraq (1992-94) and became Secretary (West) in the Ministry of External Affairs from 1998-2002.

The Canadian House of Commons honoured Mr. Kalha with a citation on June 14, 2001. The President of India appointed Mr. Kalha as a Member, National Human Rights Commission (NHRC) in 2003 on his superannuation. He presently holds the Chair of Excellence at USI.

Mr. Kalha is the author of two well-known books on Iraq and on the India-China Boundary Question.

INDEX